A
Linguistic Guide
to
Language Learning

Second Edition

A
Linguistic Guide
to
Language Learning

Second Edition

William G. Moulton

Professor of Linguistics
PRINCETON UNIVERSITY

Published by

The Modern Language Association of America

1970

Printed in the United States of America
By the George Banta Company, Inc., Menasha, Wisconsin

Contents

Foreword

Contrast is an essential condition of human experience. It is only in comparison with heat that we recognize cold, only by bitter the sweet. Recognition of this simple fact is the key both to modern linguistics and to modern criticism. In linguistics it makes use of such concepts as "distinctive contrast" and "complementary distribution," in criticism of "tension," "paradox," and "irony." But the principle is the same. No fish ever discovered water and no monolingual speaker ever understood the unique qualities of his own language.

For centuries teachers and students have recognized that one of the best ways to learn English grammar is by studying Latin. The observation is accurate. The only inaccuracy has been in supposing that it is the structure of Latin grammar itself that elucidates English, rather than realizing that it is the process of comparison that reveals to us how our own language works. This is the reason that various guidelines for the preparation of teachers of English lay such stress on the knowledge of a foreign language. No English speaker can really understand the structure of his own language except in contrast to a foreign language. He may *use* his native language as easily as he drives a car. But if he uses it badly or if anything goes wrong, he is helpless to diagnose and correct the flaw. And in relation to English, the English teacher must be the skilled mechanic and not merely the casual user.

William Moulton's book is one of the clearest and most direct introductions to the principles of language and of contrastive linguistics that has yet been written. The history of its composition will explain its fortunate tone and approach. In May of 1964 a group of linguists and English and foreign language teachers gathered in the conference room of the Modern Language Association at the instigation of Mortimer Graves, who had for years insisted that an essential purpose of language teaching, either English or foreign, should be to prepare a person to learn a foreign language on his own. Our world is contracting with frightening speed. We are now only a few hours from Europe, Asia, and

Africa. American business and education become ever more closely entwined with that of other countries. And while the rest of the world appears to be learning English faster than we are learning foreign languages, any one of us still faces the distinct possibility of finding himself living for a period of time in a country whose language he had no chance to learn in school—be it Japanese, Arabic, or Swahili. The conference decided, first, to draw up a brief statement of principles that would show how language learning in school can be made helpful to independent language learning later in life. This statement has been published (in *PMLA*, September, Part II, 1965, p. *A-8*) and we hope that it will prove useful to textbook publishers and teachers of English and the foreign languages.

The second decision was to draw up a handbook for adults who needed to learn a foreign language on their own. Various members of the conference were assigned different chapters, Mr. Moulton the chapter on linguistics. In July he went off for a year's sabbatical to Switzerland where he sat down, without his library but with only his superb knowledge, to decide how linguistic concepts could help the adult "autodidact" learn a foreign language. Before he knew it, his chapter had grown into this book, which he sent back to us with apologies and proposals for revising and cutting. The readers recognized, however, that whatever may be done for the handbook—which is still needed and still in process—the context and audience for which he was writing had led Moulton to produce a uniquely valuable introduction for the adult language learner which would also be very helpful to teachers of both English and the modern foreign languages. We are grateful to Dudley Bailey, Mortimer Graves, Albert H. Marckwardt, and Donald D. Walsh for reading the manuscript and making valuable suggestions. We are pleased that Mr. Moulton has permitted the MLA to publish the book. Our own main concern is for teachers, but we feel sure that the discussion will be equally valuable to its original audience—the layman who wishes to know something about linguistics and language learning.

28 March 1966

John H. Fisher
Executive Secretary
Modern Language Association

Preface

There is no royal road to language learning. No matter what our background, training, and previous experience, each of us will find that learning a foreign language requires time, effort, patience, and practice, practice, practice. Some of us learn more quickly than others, of course; but even the best of us cannot learn a language overnight. When we read of courses which claim to offer "French Made Easy" or some such thing, we should beware. What they teach may indeed be easy; but if it is, it is not French. For French is hard; and so is every other language—particularly the effective use of our own. When people speak of one language as being "easier" than another, what they generally refer to is the amount of effort required to gain a very elementary knowledge. It is certainly quite easy to learn a bit of a language which is closely related to one or two others we already know—to learn a useful smattering of Dutch, for example, if we already know English and German. And it seems to be true that there are languages which, at the start, are intrinsically easier than others, regardless of what we may have learned previously. (English is said by many to be a relatively "easy" language in this sense. I wouldn't know; I learned it at my mother's knee.) But if by "learning a language" we mean acquiring a control over it even vaguely comparable to our control over our native language, then it is doubtful whether one language is much easier than another. Certainly they are all hard. Learning a new one may be a stimulating and enjoyable experience, but it is bound to require a lot of work.

If learning a foreign language inevitably requires a lot of work, is there not perhaps something we can do to insure that this work will at least be as efficient as possible? The question is an important one, since it seems likely that in the coming decades more and more Americans—especially those who aspire to leading positions in the world—will need to learn more and more foreign languages. The problem is compounded by the fact that no one can predict just what language or languages he will need to know later on in life. The student who has learned French, German, Russian, or Spanish in school and college may later on find out that the language he *really* needs to know is Hindi, or Vietnamese. Is there not some kind of knowledge, some sort of linguistic sophistication, that we can give to such a person that will make the learning of *any* foreign language more efficient?

This book has been written in the belief that there *is* a kind of linguistic sophistication which, once learned, will make the learning of any foreign language less arduous, more efficient—and probably also more enjoyable. Though this is largely a matter of blind faith, let me give what little evidence I can to support it.

The most striking example I can cite is one which I experienced a number of years ago. At the opening of the fall term I discovered that I had "inherited" a graduate student in linguistics. I was to take the place of his regular adviser, who was away on leave. As we went over the student's previous work and tried to plan his studies for the coming year, I made a horrifying discovery: this young man had not yet satisfied the Ph.D. language requirement of a reading knowledge of French and German! This was both preposterous and embarrassing—preposterous because he was a student of linguistics, of all things; and embarrassing because the previous year I had nobly and eloquently upheld the value of the Ph.D. language requirement when it had come up for discussion before the faculty of the Graduate School. Aghast, I asked him how much French and/or German he knew. "None," came the disarming reply. Not that he didn't know any foreign languages. He had an excellent knowledge of New Testament Greek; he spoke fluent Spanish; he had done field work and published an article on an American Indian language; and he had just returned from an additional year of field work on a Philippine language. But French and German? No, he knew neither.

The spirit of the adviser rose within me. I told him that, by stretching things a bit, he could wait until the end of the term to take the regular examinations in French and German; and I told him that preparing for these examinations should be his primary concern during the coming months. But I need not have worried. The man carried a full load of course work, studied French and German on the side, and passed both examinations with flying colors. (I might add that the examinations were not the farce that they sometimes are. They were prepared, administered, and corrected by a faculty-wide committee; and so many students failed them that the Ph.D. language requirement was again brought up for discussion the following term.)

How did he do it? Part of the answer is that he was unquestionably a skilled and experienced language learner. But equally important—perhaps more important—was the fact that he possessed to a high degree what I have referred to above as "linguistic sophistication." He knew how human languages work. In attacking a new language he knew what things to look for and what things not to carry over from his native English. When he found, in French, that a past participle must be inflected to agree with a preceding direct object (a practice which, from the point of view of English, is unnecessary and absurd), he quickly saw the point and then quietly and efficiently went on with the job of learning. In studying German he did not fight the intricacies of word order (though he must have found them as ridiculous—from the point of view of English—as did Mark Twain); he was able to grasp the essentials quickly and again get on with the job of learning.

What must one do to acquire this sort of "linguistic sophistication"? Must we all study linguistics in graduate school, and do field work in some exotic language? I hope not. I hope that even reading the pages of this book—and of further, better books that may be written by others—will help any adult to learn a foreign language more efficiently. Nothing which I have written here will ever produce any sort of "French Made Easy." It will still be hard. But if it can be learned more efficiently, it can also be learned faster and better. And if it can be learned faster and better it will at least *seem* easier. Perhaps this book will do little to speed the learner's task, but only make the task more interesting because some new insights into human languages have been provided. Even that would be gratifying.

In writing this book I have limited myself almost entirely to the *principles* of language learning, and have said very little about *methods* of language learning. Of course, I have my own ideas about methods; but they are little more than that—just my own ideas. I have therefore thought it better to confine myself to that aspect of language learning in which I can claim some professional competence: the field of linguistics.

As John H. Fisher has written in his gracious foreword, the original stimulus for this book came from the ever stimulating Mortimer Graves, and it is to him that I gratefully dedicate it. I am also grateful to those other colleagues, mentioned in Fisher's foreword, who were kind enough to read the original manuscript and to offer many suggestions which I eagerly accepted. My special thanks go to Fisher himself—for goading me gently into writing this chapter-that-became-a-book, and for being willing to publish it under the sponsorship of the Modern Language Association.

Most of this book was written during a happy year of leave in Zurich, Switzerland, while I was the grateful recipient of a McCosh Faculty Fellowship from Princeton University and of a fellowship from the John Simon Guggenheim Memorial Foundation. Both of my benefactors supposed that I was devoting full time to a promised monograph on the vowel systems of Swiss German dialects. I hope that they, as well as my Swiss colleagues, will forgive me for having stolen time from Swiss vowels to write this linguistic guide to language learning.

William G. Moulton

Princeton, New Jersey
March 1966

Preface to the Second Edition

This new edition reflects, in a modest way, the continuing development of linguistic theory. Most of the first edition was written in 1964, at a time when grammatical transformations were considered to be meaningful. Now, some five years later, it seems preferable to assume that most of the meaning of any sentence is provided by its deep structure—which may or may not be part of the semantic component of language. The function of transformational rules is then largely one of interrelating deep structure (representing the way we understand sentences) with surface structure (representing the way we say sentences). This change in theory has led to a minor rewriting of pp. 27-28 and to a major rewriting of pp. 77-86. Otherwise the text remains unchanged, except for the replacement of two items in the bibliography.

To the language learner who looks to the linguist for guidance, this change in theory may seem insignificant. No matter. Except for rare breakthroughs, progress comes slowly—and usually in small steps. Perhaps we now understand a little bit more about language, and how to learn it, than we did five years ago. I have simply tried to add this little bit. The basic message remains unchanged.

W.G.M.

Princeton, New Jersey
August 1969

Chapter One

Language and the Learner

It is tempting to begin this book on language learning with a few
ringing slogans such as "You Too Can Learn Transylvanian,"
"Learn Burgundian in Ten Easy Lessons," or perhaps "Even Idiots
Speak Mauretanian—So Why Not You?" Instead, we shall start off
more soberly (and, we believe, more honestly) with a tale of frustra-
tion, discouragement, and humiliation.

In preparation for a trip to France, you have spent a year or
more bravely trying to learn French. Finally the great day has
come, and you are safely lodged in a little hotel in Paris. Wanting
to "see all," you wander into one of the less hygienic sections of
that lovely city. As you pass by a rather dingy alley, you notice a
group of dirty-faced children in black smocks happily playing some
sort of game. Intrigued, you stop to watch. And as you watch, a
chilling realization suddenly creeps over you: *These children are
talking French!* Not only that—they are talking it fluently and,
as far as you can judge, flawlessly. All those things that you struggled with for a year and more they say quite effortlessly. What you,
as an adult, found so hard to learn is for them—quite literally—
mere child's play.

The experience is a shattering one. And it can happen over
and over again. It has happened to the writer of these lines five
times in five different countries.

Though one is inclined to react to such an experience in terms
of blackest despair, there are a number of useful lessons which can
be learned from it. First of all, it is reassuring to know that one

1

does not need to be an intellectual giant in order to learn French, or any other language. Indeed, language learning can hardly be an "intellectual" activity at all, in the usual sense of that word, if it requires nothing more advanced than the mind of a five-year-old. A great intellect is perhaps necessary before one can say anything worth listening to; but mere talking itself, as well as learning how to talk, apparently requires little in the way of intellectual capacity. This is comforting to know.

There are also some further lessons to be gained from this experience. If small children learn languages so brilliantly, is there not perhaps something in their methods of language learning which we, as adults, can copy? There certainly is, though we must not try to push the matter too far. One of the most striking aspects of a child's language learning is the fact that he spends so much time at it. He talks with his parents, he talks with his brothers and sisters, he talks with his playmates; if no one else is around, he even talks to himself. It is a little sad to realize that the child practices so much, because this is something which no adult language learner can ever hope to match—he has too much else to do. Nevertheless, this seems to be part of the secret of language learning: it requires lots and lots of practice, lots of talking out loud.

A second thing we notice is that a child does not "fight" the language he is trying to learn: he simply copies what he hears, or says what he is told to say, without worrying about whether this seems reasonable or not. Adult learners are likely to be somewhat offended when told that the past tense of *bring* is *brought* rather than *brang;* they can become impatient when you insist that *oats* must be plural even though *wheat* is singular; and they can get downright huffy when told that *you mustn't do it* and *you don't have to do it* mean quite different things, despite the fact that the positive forms of these sentences (*you must do it, you have to do it*) do not differ in meaning at all. The adult, in short, has vast numbers of preconceived ideas about language—one of which is that every language should be "logical," and that there must be a "reason" for the way everything is said. Not so the child. He couldn't care less. He simply mimics what he hears and refuses to worry about such adult problems as "logic" and "reason." And this, apparently, is the attitude which any language learner ought to take, if we can judge by the excellent results which it produces for children.

Practice and mimicry, then, are two of the child's secret weapons in language learning, and they are two devices which the adult must copy as much as he can. But if practice and mimicry were all that one needed, language would cease to be primarily a human activity since parrots would be the greatest language learners of them all. There must be at least one more essential and exclusively human ingredient—and indeed there is. It is the ability to see patterns, to make analogies, to build new forms on the basis of old ones. We first recognize it in the child, oddly enough, when he makes mistakes—not just any mistakes, but mistakes like those in the preceding paragraph: *bring, brang* on the analogy of *sing, sang;* or *one man, two mans* on the analogy of *one pan, two pans;* or *Be careful!—I am becarefuling!* on the analogy of *Behave!—I am behaving!* Without the ability to make analogies, human beings could (like parrots) say only those things which they had learned by rote from others; *with* the ability to make analogies, even a child is able to say (theoretically) an infinite number of things which have never been said before. The use of analogy must be enormously important in language learning. Fortunately it is something which the adult can manage just as well as the child—perhaps even better.

Our episode of the little French children speaking fluent French was given to illustrate the fact that human beings at a very early age can learn to speak a language marvelously well—not perfectly, perhaps, but certainly well enough to be the envy of any foreign adult. Furthermore, they can apply this marvelous language learning ability not just to one language but, if the conditions are equally favorable, to a second, a third, perhaps even a fourth—no one really knows just how many. Many American families have had the experience of going abroad for a year or so and seeing their small children learn perfect French, Swedish, Arabic, or whatnot. And there are many documented cases of children who have spoken one language with their parents, a second with their nurse, a third with their playmates, and so on.

We have found three aspects of children's language learning which the adult can gratefully copy: practice, mimicry, and analogy. Yet we must be very careful not to press the matter too far. Those ads which invite us to "Learn Iberian as a Child Does" are really a gigantic swindle. Precisely because we *are* adults, we can never again learn a foreign language "as a child does," much as we might like to. For apparently it is the very process of becoming an adult which so conditions us that foreign languages suddenly become "foreign" and hence no longer learnable in the same way they are for children. Though this phenomenon is by no means well understood, we can at least discuss those aspects of it which are clear to any alert observer.

How long do children retain their ability to learn a language, under the proper conditions, perfectly and (so it would seem) effortlessly? Though there are individual exceptions, by and large it seems to last up to about the age of twelve to fourteen. Then some drastic changes take place—swiftly in some cases, more slowly in others. On the one hand, the child (assuming he is an American) develops a new attitude toward English: where it was previously simply *a* language, it now becomes *the* language—against which all others are measured. At the same time, the child also develops a new attitude toward all languages *other* than English. Where their sounds and forms and meanings were previously accepted without question, they are now topics for comment and matters of ridicule or embarrassment, for they have suddenly become "foreign." Where the child of six or eight imitates a French uvular *r* quite unselfconsciously, the child of fourteen or sixteen looks upon it as something strange and somehow slightly improper. When asked to imitate it, he may blush or stammer or giggle; and though he may actually be able to pronounce it with ease in isolated words, when he says full sentences he will most likely replace it with the familiar *r* of his American English. What a difference there is between the six-year-old's unquestioning acceptance of the foreign language just as it comes, and the sixteen-year-old's awkward insistence on turning everything back into English!

One's first reaction to this change which comes over children during their early teens is one of regret. How sad that the young child's marvelous language learning ability is now lost forever! Indeed it is sad; but it is also probably necessary and desirable. For losing this early language learning ability seems to be part and parcel of the very desirable process of becoming an adult. Where the child is plastic, malleable, still easily formed and shaped, we wish the adult to be fixed and, in a sense, rigid—with well-formed ideas as to what is right or wrong, proper or improper, reasonable or unreasonable. Though we want him to be open-minded toward new ideas, we also want him to have firm values and standards to judge them by, so that he can decide on his own whether he should accept them or not. Every normal person goes through such a "hardening"

process to a greater or lesser extent, and as part of it—apparently
—he loses the young child's chameleonlike acceptance of any and
all languages. From now on, English is the "standard" from which
all other languages are judged, and life itself is thought to have the
form and contours which the English language gives to it.

To compensate for the loss of perfect language learning ability, the transition from childhood to early adulthood fortunately
brings with it two great gains. First, though the young adult may
have to work harder to learn a foreign language, he also remembers
it much better. With small children it is a case of "easy come, easy
go." The six-year-old who learned Dutch so marvelously during
that half year his family was in Holland may have forgotten nearly
every word of Dutch by the time another six months have rolled by.
Or, if he stays in Holland without his family, he will soon forget
every bit of his English. Not so with a sixteen-year-old. He, too, can
of course forget the French which he laboriously learned in high
school; but he forgets it at a far slower rate, and some of it will
stick with him forever. As for his native English, only under the
most unusual circumstances will he ever forget enough to hamper
his speaking it fluently.

The second great gain of early adulthood is, as far as language
learning is concerned, a mixed blessing. Though small children are
notorious for asking constant questions concerning the world about
them ("Why is the sky blue? Why is grass green?"), they are also
easily satisfied and will accept answers such as that "the moon is
made of green cheese." Young adults, on the other hand, begin to
insist more and more on answers which "make sense" because they
tie in with the many other things which they are learning. In the
case of a foreign language, they want especially to know why it behaves so often in ways which are at odds with the "normal," "reasonable," English way of handling things. Unfortunately there is no
way of giving a quick and easy answer which "makes sense" to
them. As the great linguist Leonard Bloomfield once remarked:
"When anyone asks you *why* the Russians (or whoever) talk the
way they do, the only real answer you can give is: the little ones do
because the big ones do. That's just the way the language is." But
this, of course, is a "green cheese" type of answer, and adults—precisely because they are adults—find it hard to accept. They still
want to know "why" the foreign language is different from English.

Though the adult's continuous insistence on "reasonable" answers is in many ways a hindrance, it can also be of great benefit if it is guided in the proper channels. Where the child, it seems, can learn a foreign language *only* through imitation and analogy, the adult can also learn it through explanation and instruction. He can be told how the sounds of the foreign language are produced, how its sentences are constructed, and how its meanings are shaped. This is what any grammar book tries to do. Beyond this, the adult need no longer learn by analogy in the relatively hit-or-miss fashion of the child, but can be led skillfully into correct analogies through a series of carefully constructed drills. This is what any graded textbook tries to do. Most important, perhaps, the intellectually mature adult can also be given information of a wider scope: what human language is, and how it works. This is what the present book will try to do.

Chapter Two

Some Misconceptions

In the course of the preceding chapter we discussed briefly the one misconception which, more than all others, plagues the adult language learner: the naive but understandable belief that the English way of handling language is the only reasonable and natural one. Though it is relatively easy to rid oneself of this misconception intellectually, it is next to impossible for an adult to free himself from it entirely in practice. Try as we may, we will tend to hear and produce the sounds of the foreign language in terms of English sounds (using, for example, an English *r* or *l* in place of that Japanese sound which seems perversely to lie right between the two); we will tend to manipulate the foreign grammar as if it were English grammar (struggling, for example, to find the equivalent of *he does not live here,* when in fact the foreign language may have only the equivalent of *he lives here not*); and we will tend to handle foreign meanings as if they were English meanings (forgetting, for example, that French uses one word—*campagne*—for "he lives in the *country*" but quite another word—*pays*—for "he lives in another *country*"). Though there is no guaranteed way of overcoming difficulties of this sort, it seems clear that every adult learner must be made aware of precisely the *differences* between English and the foreign language he is learning, and that a good deal of his learning time should be spent in practicing just these differences. Where two languages agree, there is little to be learned; it is the differences which present the greatest learning problem and require the most careful practice.

Though this first misconception will be with us always and must constantly be fought against, there are a number of others which are easier to get rid of. We shall discuss here those which seem to be most widespread. Not all of them are shared equally by all adult learners, and there are surely others which could be added to the list.

Language and logic. This is largely a variation of the first misconception (that foreign languages really ought to behave like English), since we tend to equate "logic" with the English way of handling things. For example, we consider it only "logical" that, in referring to objects in the world about us, we should constantly make a distinction between singular and plural: *tree* vs. *trees, hat* vs. *hats,* etc. For speakers of some languages this is highly "illogical": the "logical" thing to do is to make a difference between singular and plural only in those few cases when it is for some reason or other particularly relevant. Why say *three hats* (with -*s*) when the idea of "plural" is expressed already, and far more accurately, by the word *three?* In English we consider it "logical" that time should be divided into past, present, and future, and we point with pride to the way our language does just this: past *the dog ate the meat,* present *the dog eats the meat,* future *the dog will eat the meat.* In part this is sheer delusion, since a "present tense" sentence such as *dogs eat meat* is really timeless and refers neither to past, present, nor future —or, if you wish, refers equally to all three. Speakers of some languages would consider our constant preoccupation with time to be highly "illogical"; they would find it far more "logical" to note whether an action is completed or left incomplete, whether it occurs just once or repeatedly, and so on. In English we think it "logical" that the word *two* means the same thing in *two dogs* and *two days;* this is even "mathematically logical." But speakers of some languages would consider this hopelessly "illogical," since the two *two*'s are so utterly different: *two dogs* can exist side by side, at the same time; but *two days* can only follow one another, and never exist side by side. Surely it is "illogical" to use the same word *two* for these very different meanings!

Even if we leave foreign languages aside and compare English only with itself, we find countless examples of the "illogical." We always make a clear distinction between "I *buy* it from you" and "you *sell* it to me"; why don't we make a similarly "logical"

8

distinction between "I *rent* it from you" and "you *rent* it to me"? Or between "I *lease* it from you" and "you *lease* it to me"? (Legal English, to be sure, can make such a distinction by using the words *lessee* and *lessor*—though most of us can never remember which means which.) In English we can shorten a phrase such as *he is not* either to *he's not* or to *he isn't*. "Logically" there surely ought to be a difference between the two, and yet there does not seem to be one; they apparently mean exactly the same thing.

Though we could pursue this matter of "logic" in language indefinitely, perhaps the above examples will suffice to make the point that logic and language have nothing to do with each other. No language is either "logical" or "illogical"; it is simply what it is, without regard to logic. We may of course prefer to think of our own language as "logical" and of other languages as "illogical" in varying degrees, depending upon how far they deviate from English. But this is mere self-delusion.

Language and Latin. For over a thousand years after the fall of the Roman Empire, Latin continued to function as the international language of the Western World and, above all, as the language of learning. It occupied a central position in the school curriculum (for the few who actually went to school), and anyone who aspired to genuine learning was expected not only to be able to read it but also to write it, to speak it, and to understand it. As a result of its pre-eminence, Latin was looked upon as *the* language par excellence, while local languages (still not national in scope) were considered crude and clumsy. Furthermore, there was for Latin a carefully worked out grammar, dating back to classical times; and because no such descriptions existed for the so-called "vernaculars" (the languages of everyday speech), they were often thought to have no grammar at all and to be little more than the formless jabberings of the uneducated. This attitude changed when such languages as French, English, Spanish, German, and Italian gradually took on standardized national forms. But when scholars then turned to the task of writing grammars for these "new" languages, they described them largely from the point of view of Latin rather than in terms of the languages themselves.

The medieval tradition of giving to Latin a central place in the school curriculum was transplanted from England to America, and it survived for a long time in gradually modified form; it was given up only recently—much to the detriment of education, as many of us would say. Despite the decrease in the study of Latin, however, the tradition of describing all other languages in terms of Latin continued to survive. One often hears, especially from the highly educated, such statements as: "I never really understood English grammar until I studied Latin." This can only mean that the "English" grammar which such a person failed at first to understand was strongly influenced and distorted by Latin Grammar. Such a grammar is obviously not fully comprehensible until one *does* study Latin. If it were a genuine "English" grammar, it could by definition be understood in terms of English and of English alone.

What do we mean by a grammar which is presented "from the point of view of Latin," or which is "strongly influenced and distorted by Latin grammar"? Because the traditional Latinate grammar of English (now largely abandoned) is still too close to many of us, it will be more instructive to start off with an example from a completely foreign language. Not long ago the writer came upon a "modern" grammar of Japanese which "conjugated" the Japanese verb meaning 'to say' in the present tense as follows:

hanasimasu 'I say'	hanasimasu 'we say'
hanasimasu 'you say'	hanasimasu 'you say'
hanasimasu 'he says'	hanasimasu 'they say'

The verb *hanasimasu* is not in any sense irregular or exceptional; *all* Japanese verbs behave in this way.

What is wrong with this presentation of the Japanese verb? Why does it strike most of us as ludicrous? Clearly the author of this grammar had not tried to find out and describe how a *Japanese* verb behaves; instead, he based his presentation on some such *Latin* model as:

dīcō 'I say'	dīcimus 'we say'
dīcis 'you say'	dīcitis 'you say'
dīcit 'he says'	dīcunt 'they say'

This presentation of the present tense of a Latin verb is in the grand tradition of a two-thousand-year-old grammar, and it is entirely correct: the present indicative active of a Latin verb really *does* show six clearly different forms, based on distinctions of person (1st person, 2nd person, 3rd person) and number (singular, plural). This, then, is its proper "conjugation." But a Japanese verb is *never* conjugated for person and number; it always shows only one form where Latin shows six. This is not to say that a Japanese verb is not "conjugated" in other ways. It has, among a distressing number of other forms, a present *hanasimasu* and a past *hanasimasita;* and one might even go so far as to say that it is conjugated for "politeness": polite *hanasimasu,* plain *hanasu.* But *no* Japanese verb is *ever* conjugated in *any* form for person (1st, 2nd, 3rd) or number (singular, plural).

With this Japanese example as an introduction, let us now consider the traditional "conjugation" of a sample English verb in the present and past tenses:

Present:	I speak	we speak	*Past:*	I spoke	we spoke
	you speak	you speak		you spoke	you spoke
	he speaks	they speak		he spoke	they spoke

In the past tense this "conjugation" is obviously just as absurd as the Japanese example: with one exception (*was, were*), all English verbs show only a single form in the past; there is no conjugation for person and number whatever. The present tense is not much different: again with one exception (*am, is, are*), no English verb shows more than two different forms (*speak, speaks*), and some half a dozen auxiliary verbs (*can, may, will, shall, must, ought,* and under certain conditions *need* and *dare*) show only one form. To present the "conjugation" of English verbs in the above manner is simply to project upon them the structure of the Latin verb. If we teach a foreigner to "conjugate" the past tense of an English verb by having him rattle off such a series as "I spoke, you spoke, he spoke, we spoke, you spoke, they spoke," we are teaching him nothing whatever about the verb; we are merely giving him an exercise in the pronunciation of pronouns.

In times past it was not uncommon to find English grammars which "declined" the English noun as follows:

Nominative	the table	(mēnsa)
Genitive	of the table	(mēnsae)
Dative	to the table	(mēnsae)
Accusative	the table	(mēnsam)
Ablative	by or from the table	(mēnsā)
Vocative	O table!	(mēnsa)

These six "cases" obviously have nothing whatever to do with English but are taken from the Latin model given in parentheses at the right; and even in the case of Latin it is absurd to include here a "vocative" *mēnsa*, since such a form would hardly occur. (Winston Churchill is said to have balked at the study of Latin because he refused to learn a language which used such a ridiculous form as *mēnsa* 'O table!'.)

Though this "declension" of the English noun has now been abandoned, it is still not uncommon to find grammars which struggle bravely to find in English the same six tenses which occur in Latin:

Present	I love	(amō)
Imperfect	I was loving	(amābam)
Future	I shall love	(amābō)
Perfect	I have loved	(amāvī)
Pluperfect	I had loved	(amāveram)
Future Perfect	I shall have loved	(amāverō)

This analysis is again entirely correct for Latin, which has precisely the six tenses given to the right, in parentheses; but it has little or nothing to do with English. In English we have a present (*love*) and a past (*loved*); we also have such phrasal forms as *do/did love, is/was loving, have/had loved, have/had been loving,* as well as such further phrasal forms as *shall/should love, will/would love, can/could love, shall/should be loving, will/would be loving, can/could be loving, shall/should have loved, will/would have loved, can/could have loved, shall/should have been loving, will/would have been loving, can/could have been loving,* plus similar variants of *may/might love, must love, ought to love,* etc. There is certainly no dearth of such forms in English. Yet no matter how we twist our two tenses and many phrases, we can never come out with the same six forms as Latin. An analysis which tries to do so is presented "from the point of view of Latin," and is "strongly influenced and distorted by Latin grammar."

What should we conclude from this review of "Latinate" Japanese and English grammar? It seems clear that a grammarian should analyze the language he is describing in its own terms and not in those of Latin, and that a learner should accept such a language as it actually is and not expect it to behave like Latin. There is nothing "queer" about a language simply because it does not decline its nouns and conjugate its verbs as Latin does. It may, by sheer chance, have the same three genders as Latin (masculine, feminine, neuter); but it may also have six genders or, more likely, none at all. If it has cases similar to those of Latin, there is no reason why the grammarian must present them in the Latin order "nominative, genitive, dative, accusative, ablative" (an order which, as a matter of fact, makes singularly little sense even in Latin); there may be good reasons for presenting them in the order "nominative, accusative, dative, genitive," or in some other sequence. Many of us love Latin and are fascinated by the unique role which it has played in the history of our civilization. In terms of grammar, however, it is just another language; and we are no more justified in distorting other languages to make them fit the grammar of Latin than we would be in distorting them to fit the grammar of Choctaw.

Language and writing. For the normal adult—especially the highly educated adult—language exists in two separate though obviously related forms: speech and writing. If asked to rate the two in order of priority, we tend to think of writing as primary, and of speech as derived and hence secondary. After all, writing is permanent and enduring, and can be handed down unchanged through the ages; whereas speech is evanescent and transitory, and disappears almost as soon as it is uttered (or at least it did before the advent of the phonograph and the tape recorder). Though writing can be thought of as a way of putting speech down on paper, it seems more reasonable to think of speech as a way of expressing writing in audible form. When we hear someone use a new word, we inevitably want to know—besides its meaning—how it is spelled. When we question the spelling of such a word as *often,* we seldom ask, "Why isn't it spelled the way it's pronounced?" but more often, "Why isn't it pronounced the way it's spelled?" And when students are introduced to a foreign language by means of a phonetic transcription, they soon begin to fret and ask: "When will we get the *real* language?"—that is, the customary spelling. For most of us, writing actually *does* seem to be the "real language," and speech only a pale and fleeting reflection of it.

This is one way of looking at speech and writing. But we can also take another view. If we consider the world about us, we find that all of mankind beyond infancy can speak and understand, but that less than half of it can read and write. If we look at the languages of the world, we find that only a small fraction of them (all the important ones, to be sure) are recorded in writing. And if we look back into history, we find that man has been speaking and understanding for half a million to a million years, but that he has been using writing for at most one per cent of that time. From this broader point of view it seems clear that language is essentially and necessarily speech, and only incidentally and by no means necessarily writing. In this day and age when perhaps half the adults in the world can read and write, we tend to forget that writing in anything approaching the modern sense was invented only some five thousand years ago, and that until very recently it was the cherished possession of only a tiny fraction of the world's population.

There is still a third way of looking at speech and writing: from the point of view of the language learner. It is entirely possible to learn a foreign language without knowing anything of the way it is written; indeed, this is the way most foreign language learning goes on in the world—to say nothing of native language learning. It is of course also possible to learn to speak *and* to read a foreign language; this is obviously the way our literate society handles foreign language learning in schools and colleges. On the other hand, it is next to impossible to learn *only* to read and write a foreign language, without hearing or speaking it at all. If the reader doubts the truth of this statement, let him test it by getting, say, a grammar of Hungarian and trying to learn the language without using any sounds at all. He will soon find that it just can't be done. Not knowing how Hungarian is pronounced by the Hungarians, he will inevitably start using his own private pronunciations—silently, perhaps, but they will be "internal pronunciations" nonetheless. To learn a language without writing it is easy; this is what most of the world does. But to learn a language without speaking it is an enormously difficult, almost inhuman task.

From the point of view of the language learner, there is one further remark which should be made about the importance of speech. When the typical school or college student learns a foreign language, he is inclined to study it in much the same way he does his history or English: he goes home, reads the book, and tries to understand the ideas which are presented in it. Though this may be admirable for other subjects, it is hopelessly inadequate for a foreign language, since here he must not only understand the ideas but also learn the language at the same time. As he reads, silently, he will inevitably use "internal pronunciations" whether he thinks he is doing so or not. If these are his own "private pronunciations," the results are ridiculous: no one will be able to understand him later on when he tries to talk out loud. Since some kind of pronunciation has to be used in any case, it obviously should be as close an approximation of the foreign pronunciation as possible. But even if the student uses a flawless "silent" pronunciation, his study habits are hopelessly inefficient. Reading silently, he will be using only his visual memory. By reading out loud, he can first double his efficiency through adding auditory memory. At the same time he will also add motor memory, and this will at least quadruple his efficiency because it is by far the most efficient memory of all. (Motor memory, we may recall, is the memory of what we do with our muscles. Proof of its efficiency is the fact that nobody ever forgets how to ride a bicycle even though he may have had a terrible time learning it in the first place.) All the evidence we have thus indicates that a learner should look at a foreign language primarily as something which is spoken, and only secondarily as something which is written; and this seems to be true even if his ultimate goal is only a reading knowledge of the language in question.

At the beginning of this section we pointed out that most persons look at writing as primary and speech as secondary, whereas we now seem to have reached precisely the opposite conclusion. What is the true relationship between the two? Since speech can exist freely without writing, whereas writing (in any normal sense of the term) has never been known to exist without speech (either now or, as in the case of Latin, at some time in the past), it seems clear that speech must be primary and writing secondary; and this is certainly the best viewpoint for any language learner to adopt. On the other hand, it is also true that once a written form of a language has evolved, it tends to some extent to develop into a special language of its own, partly divorced from speech. Written English is by no means identical with spoken English, and written French or German or Italian is by no means identical with the spoken forms of these languages. For example, if a person should talk in sentences like those of this book, his speech would sound—precisely—"bookish." Though there are many levels of speech, from the highly informal to the highly formal, even the most formal variety is unlike normal written English. (We exclude here the case of a speaker who reads from a manuscript. This is not "spoken English" but rather written English made audible.) Learning to read written French (or Russian or Spanish) is, fortunately, a relatively simple matter once one knows how to speak and understand the language. Learning to write it in its conventional written form, however, is a vastly more complicated process. Though all of us know spoken English marvelously well by the time we enter school, we spend a good part of the next twelve years learning the proper form of written English— some of us with more success, some with less. We cannot expect to learn to write another language properly (except in its simplest forms, as in personal letters) without a comparable amount of training.

Language and grammar. In order to know a foreign language, it is obvious that we have to know its grammar. Many adults, however, suffer from a grave misconception as to what the expression "know grammar" means. Very often they believe that it means, first, the ability to recite vast numbers of paradigms such as, for French, *je parle, tu parles, il parle, nous parlons, vous parlez, ils parlent* 'I speak, you speak, he speaks, we speak, you speak, they speak.' And they believe that it means, second, the ability to make vast numbers of statements about the way a language behaves, such as, for French again: "An adjective must agree in gender and number with the noun it modifies," in order to "explain" such things as *le manteau est vert* 'the overcoat is green,' *la robe est verte* 'the dress is green,' *les manteaux sont verts* 'the overcoats are green,' *les robes sont vertes* 'the dresses are green'—where the word for 'green' appears (when written) in four different shapes. Some adults doggedly *do* learn to make such statements, though most give up after a short time with the despairing remark: "How can I possibly learn French grammar when I don't really even know *English* grammar?"

"Knowing grammar" in this analytical sense is of course necessary for a teacher, since we expect him to be able to give all possible help to his students. But "knowing grammar" is for the learner something quite different again. He needs to "know grammar" only in the sense of being able to apply it—to "perform" it or "behave" it. In this sense we all "know" English grammar marvelously well, since we can apply it to understand what others say and to produce ourselves an endless number of grammatically correct sentences. Precisely this way of "knowing grammar" is what we also need in order to speak and understand a foreign language. If a learner then wants to take the further step of learning paradigms and explanations, he may of course do so; this is his choice. This further step is by no means necessary, and it may or may not be helpful, depending on the individual.

Of what use are "paradigms," such as *je parle, tu parles,* etc.? Some people find comfort and reassurance in them, and for such they may be very useful. But there is also a certain danger in them. If a person knows *only* paradigms, then when he wants to say 'they speak' in French he will have to run through the whole paradigm until he finally comes to the proper form: *ils parlent.* No one can speak a foreign language this way. If one has only a limited amount of time available (and who of us has *unlimited* time?), it is far better to spend it in practicing pattern drills. Here the learner takes a model sentence, such as *Je parle français* 'I speak French,' and then practices it with different subjects, not in any fixed order: *Il parle français* 'He speaks French,' *Vous parlez français* 'You speak French,' *Henri parle français* 'Henry speaks French,' *Nous parlons français* 'We speak French,' etc. This is the way language actually works, and this is the way it should be practiced.

Of what use are "explanations," such as: "An adjective must agree in gender and number with the noun it modifies"? Here adult learners vary enormously. Some—the lucky few—are able to take the language just as it comes, without "fighting" it. Most of us, however, again need comfort and reassurance. When a language behaves differently from English we want to know "why" it does so. No one, of course, can really tell us "why." There is no reason under the sun "why" a French adjective must agree in gender and number with the noun it modifies; this is just the way the language works. Instead of being "explanations," such statements are merely generalizations on the behavior of the language; and it is this behavior that we really need to learn. We need, for example, to be able to give quickly and automatically such responses as the following:

Stimulus: le manteau   *Response:* Le manteau est vert.
           la robe   La robe est verte.
           le chapeau   Le chapeau est vert.
           la table   La table est verte.

"Explanations" are useful only to the extent that they really do help us to learn such responses more efficiently.

Language and vocabulary. Where some adults think of language learning as primarily a matter of learning "grammar," others go to the opposite extreme and think of it as primarily a matter of learning "vocabulary"—as if a language were little more than a bag of words. Yet all of us know that it is perfectly possible to understand all the words in a sentence of a foreign language and still not know what the sentence means. Knowing words is not enough; one also has to know how the language groups them together, by means of its grammar.

With these remarks we do not mean to underestimate the matter of vocabulary learning; it is a very serious problem for any language learner. How is it best accomplished? During early stages of language learning the best method discovered thus far is to have the learner use the vocabulary actively by memorizing and acting out brief dialogues and the like. Here the emphasis is on actually *using* and *living* the language, rather than on memorizing huge lists of words with their translations. Instead of memorizing (for French) "*chapeau* equals *hat*," the learner really uses the word in such sentences as perhaps: *Où est mon chapeau?* 'Where's my hat?' and *Quel joli chapeau!* 'What a pretty hat!'

It is in later stages of language learning, especially when one begins to read, that vocabulary learning becomes a serious problem. Though everyone has to work out his own best method of learning new words, there are three devices which can be recommended. First, never "look a word up" until you have read the whole context in which it occurs—at least an entire sentence. Very often the context will make the meaning quite clear. Second, don't be afraid of making "intelligent guesses." This is the way you learned most of the words you know in English, rather than by looking them up in a dictionary. Third, make a special list of your "nuisance words"— the ones you find yourself looking up over and over again. Put them down on paper and memorize them. This is probably the only time you will be justified in writing out a list of words and memorizing them blindly; otherwise this procedure is pretty much a waste of time.

Language and translation. Still other adults tend to think of language learning as primarily a matter of translation. In one of its forms—translating from English into the foreign language—this leads to what has been called the "cookbook method" of language learning. The student is first given a recipe (grammatical rules) and some ingredients (new vocabulary), and he is then told to bake a cake (write out translations of sentences from English into the foreign language). The results are usually atrocious. What the student typically receives is practice not in writing *correct* French (or whatever) but rather practice in writing *incorrect* French. Language teachers are now agreed that, except in truly advanced language instruction, students should be asked to write in the foreign language only those things which they already know how to say orally. Otherwise language learning degenerates into a puzzle-solving activity.

Translation in the opposite direction, from the foreign language into English, avoids some of the errors of the "cookbook method" since here the student at least does not receive practice in distorting the foreign language. At really advanced levels of language instruction, translation of this sort can be a very useful exercise—though of course it forces the student to spend at least as much time in perfecting his control of English as in enlarging his knowledge of the foreign language. (It is splendid for the student to do this; we should merely realize that he is then devoting only half his time to foreign language learning.) At elementary levels of language instruction, however, translation from the foreign language into English is apt to degenerate into little more than a kind of deciphering process. Instead of working within the foreign language as much as possible, the student here tries to get away from the foreign language and back into English again, as quickly as he can. This is of course absurd. The whole purpose of foreign language learning is to enable the student to work as completely as possible *within* the foreign language, without reference to English. Translation is precisely what he must learn to overcome.

How can one learn a foreign language—especially the reading of a foreign language—*without* constant translation? We have suggested above that a learner should start out speaking the language, memorizing and acting out brief dialogues, and learning by analogy through practice with pattern drills. Translation of a sort is involved here, since the learner must of course know the meaning of what he is saying; but this is very different from translating in the cookbook or deciphering sense. For the student who has achieved an elementary knowledge in this way and then wishes to gain a reading knowledge, the late Eduard Prokosch used to advocate a method which the writer and many others have found extremely useful. He called it "reading in three concentric circles." Start out with perhaps half a page of text and examine it thoroughly, from every point of view. In this innermost circle, look up every word you do not really know and check on every point of grammar. Then proceed to the next circle: for about a page and a half, make sure that you understand every sentence and look up every word which you cannot reasonably guess at, but do no more than this. Finally, in the outermost and largest circle, read through eight or ten pages without looking up anything at all. Force yourself to make intelligent guesses as to the meaning of words and grammatical constructions. Then read through these same eight or ten pages again, and stop to look things up only where you understand absolutely nothing at all. All three of these "concentric circles" give you valuable training. In the innermost circle you learn both grammar and vocabulary; in the middle circle you take grammar for granted and concentrate on vocabulary; in the outermost circle you take both for granted and concentrate primarily on fluency and comprehension through intelligent guessing. All three steps are necessary, and all three can be accomplished without translation in the deciphering sense.

Language and nationality. In a discussion of common misconceptions about language learning we need to mention, finally, two which are often used as excuses to avoid language learning. The first has to do with nationality. One often hears it said that "Americans are poor language learners," whereas the Russians (or the Dutch, or whatnot) "are a nation of gifted language learners." What truth is there in statements of this sort?

Let's look at the facts. We have already seen that language learning requires an intellectual capacity equivalent to that of a five-year-old child. Surely the Americans, who lead the world in many fields of humanistic and scientific endeavor, do not lag behind other nations on this score. Could it be that we have speech organs that are somehow different from those of other nations? Surely this is also absurd. All human beings are born with identical language-speaking equipment. There is no such thing as a Russian larynx, a German tongue, or (in language, at least) a French palate. An American child brought up in Rome, Moscow, or Tokyo will learn Italian, Russian, or Japanese just as well as his playmates in those cities. Intellectually and physiologically he is just as well equipped as they are.

If Americans do not differ intellectually or physiologically from the people of other nations, could it be that they differ psychologically? To the extent that Americans really *are* "poor language learners," the reason does indeed seem to be psychological. In many countries of the world a person who aspires to a position of learning and prestige knows from the very start that he must learn one or more foreign languages. To give just one example: a Dutch child who plans to attend a university knows that, to be admitted, he must learn no less than five foreign languages, usually Greek, Latin, English, French, and German—besides, of course, written Dutch. This seems a natural thing to do because he is literally surrounded by foreign languages: a trip of a few score miles will take him in one direction to England, in another to France, in a third to Germany; and a flip of the radio dial will bring him a program in any one of half a dozen or more foreign languages. Beyond this, knowing foreign languages is in educated circles simply "the thing to do." *Not* to know any English, French, or German would be rather humiliating.

The psychological situation in the United States is vastly different from this. First, it is entirely possible to attain a position of learning with only a minimal knowledge of one or two foreign languages; and one can attain other positions of highest prestige with no knowledge of any foreign language at all. Second, one can travel hundreds—even thousands—of miles and never have to use any language but English; and if one turns on the radio and hears, say, German, it simply means that one has by error tuned in on a program of the local German singing society. Third, instead of bringing prestige, knowledge of a foreign language is more likely to indicate that one is an as yet unassimilated immigrant. Knowledge of a foreign language is in this sense something to be *overcome* rather than something to be *acquired*. (In citing these common American attitudes toward foreign languages, we are merely trying to give a realistic appraisal of the facts as they are. We do not mean to imply that these attitudes are in any sense admirable; indeed, we find them quite mistaken—and deplorable.)

This picture of the psychological situation in the United States is perhaps an exaggerated one, since it is true that foreign languages have long been taught in our schools and colleges and that enrollments have greatly increased in recent years. Nevertheless, the student who has not been brought up in an environment where a foreign language is something one naturally *wants* to learn cannot help feeling that his foreign language course is a bit out of touch with reality—somewhat like an idle game. His teachers thus have a double task: both that of teaching him the language and that of making him feel that learning it is worth the effort.

Anyone who has taken the trouble to buy this book must surely *want* to learn a foreign language. Let him be assured that he possesses all the intellectual and physiological equipment and, since he *has* bought the book, all the psychological motivation which are required for this task.

Language and music. When people run across someone who is reported to be able to speak Swahili (or whatever) practically like a native, they very commonly remark: "Oh, then you really must be gifted musically." This is of course flattering to the supposed linguistic and musical genius. But the second part of the remark is far more revealing, because such people then always go on to say: "That's why I could never even learn French. I guess I must be practically tone deaf." Here a (supposed) lack of musical ability is used as an excuse to explain lack of success in foreign-language learning.

Is there any truth in this belief that musical ability and language-learning ability go hand in hand? Fortunately it is very easy to test. If it were true, then every great musician would also be a great language learner. This is clearly not the case, as anyone can testify who has talked with foreign musicians in the United States. They can murder English as well as musical morons. It would be interesting to discover how a theory so easy to refute ever became so widespread.

Chapter Three

How Language Works

In order to understand something of the nature of language and how it works, we can begin by examining a sample speech event and considering the elements of which it is composed. Let us assume that we have a speaker A and a hearer B; that A says something to B (just what he says is not important for our purposes); and that B understands him without difficulty. Here an act of communication has taken place. But *how* did it take place? What went on inside of A? How did the communication move from A to B? And then what went on inside of B? If we break the whole process down into successive stages, there seem to be at least eleven of them, as follows:

Encoding the message	{ 1. Semantic encoding. 2. Grammatical encoding. 3. Phonological encoding.
Sending	{ 4. From brain to speech organs. 5. Movements of the speech organs.
Transmission	6. Vibrations of the air molecules.
Receiving	{ 7. Vibrations of the ear. 8. From ear to brain.
Decoding the message	{ 9. Phonological decoding. 10. Grammatical decoding. 11. Semantic decoding.

We need to consider each of these stages, one by one. The most interesting stages are of course those which go on inside A's and B's heads; and yet these are precisely the ones that we cannot observe directly. Nevertheless, if we construct a simple but comprehensive theory that accounts for all the things we *can* observe, we shall probably come pretty close to what goes on in A's and B's heads— though not, of course, to the actual physical mechanisms.

1. Semantic encoding. We shall assume, first of all, that A has some sort of "idea" or "thought" or "meaning" that he wants to communicate to B. (Why A should have this idea in the first place is the biggest question of all. Fortunately, it need not concern us here. As students of language we can simply assume that A has such an idea and see where he goes from there.) The task that now faces A is: How can he get this idea into such a shape that it can be communicated in the language he is using? Let us suppose (to use the favorite example for this sort of thing) that he wants to describe the color of some object. We all know that, within the color spectrum, there is an infinite variety of shades. And yet, if A is speaking English, the spectrum has not an infinite number of colors but only six: red, orange, yellow, green, blue, violet (or, for those who learned it in the other familiar order, seven: violet, indigo, blue, green, yellow, orange, red). By this we do not mean to imply that, within the range of the spectrum, English has only six (or seven) color names. It has many more; but only these six (or seven) are basic. If, for example, we ask an English speaker about the colors "scarlet," "crimson," "carmine," or "cerise," he can describe them as various shades of "red"; but if we ask him about "red," about all he can say is: "Red is red." Does this mean that the spectrum *really* has six (or seven) basic colors? No; but the English language does. Other languages have five, four, or even three.

If, as a speaker of English, A wants to describe the color of some object, he must first shape his idea so that it will fit into the semantic system of English color terms. Since this is like putting a message into the proper shape to fit the code in which it is to be sent, we can call the process "semantic encoding." In effect, *every* message first has to undergo semantic encoding before it can be sent. Since it is often hard to see this within our own language, it may be helpful to compare English with a few other languages. In Russian, that part of a person's body which extends from his shoulder to his fingertips is encoded as *ruká;* we cannot encode it this way in English but must split it up into an *arm* and a *hand.* In German, a device which tells you what time it is is called an *Uhr* (in Spanish, it is called a *reloj*); in English we have to break this up into two semantic units, depending on whether it hangs on the wall or stands on a table (a *clock*), or is carried in the pocket or worn on the wrist (a *watch*).

In the two cases just mentioned we have the disturbing feeling that Russian and German are somehow grouping together two different "things" which ought by rights to be kept separate; but this, of course, is only because we are speakers of English. (Who knows how many different "things" a *ruká* really consists of? Or how many different kinds of objects make up an *Uhr* or a *reloj?*) Just as often, we in English use one semantic unit where other languages use two or more. In English we can *know*₁ a man and also *know*₂ where he lives; but in Spanish, French, and German, *know*₁ is (respectively) *conocer, connaître, kennen,* whereas *know*₂ is *saber, savoir, wissen.* What in English is a *map* is in German either a *Plan* (for a city) or a *Karte* (for a province or country). On the other hand, a German *Plan* is also an English *plan,* and a German *Karte* is also an English *card* or *ticket;* though a *ticket* is also a German *Billett.* The possibilities are practically limitless. In English, if we want to know someone's name, we ask: *What's your name?* In French one says what sounds to us like "How you call you?" (*Comment vous appelez-vous?*), in Italian "How self calls?" (*Come si chiama?*), in Spanish "How self calls you?" (*¿Cómo se llama usted?*), and in Russian "How you they-call?" (*Kák vás zovút?*). Spanish distinguishes given names (*nombres*) from family names (*apellidos*); Russian distinguishes between the first name or *ím'a* (e.g. *Igor*), the patronymic or *ótchestvo* (e.g. *Petrovich*), and the family name or *fam'íl'iya* (e.g. *Ilyin*). There is no single "name" in Spanish or Russian any more than there is a single *ruká* in English.

Using a bold and imprecise metaphor, we can think of every language as a vast sieve with thousands of semantic slots in it. Any idea that we want to express in that language first has to be put through this sieve. If we want to talk about colors of the spectrum, English offers six (or seven) slots, other languages offer five, four, or three. If we want to talk about a certain area of the body, Russian offers one slot (*ruká*), English two (*arm* vs. *hand*). If we want to talk about timepieces, German and Spanish offer one slot (*Uhr, reloj*), English two (*clock* vs. *watch*). If we want to talk about knowledge of people and facts, English offers one slot (*to know*), Spanish two (*conocer* vs. *saber*—and similarly French and German). If we want to talk about names, English offers one slot (*name*), Spanish two (*nombre* vs. *apellido*), Russian three (*ím'a* vs. *ótchestvo* vs. *fam'í-l'iya*). And if we want to *ask* someone his name, every language offers its own particular semantic solution.

(In the above discussion we have assumed that it is possible for people to have "ideas" which exist outside of language. There is some evidence against this belief: every time we try to do any serious thinking, we start talking to ourselves—silently, usually, but talking nonetheless. There is also some evidence to support this belief: probably all of us have had the experience of knowing what we wanted to say but not being able to find the right words to say it. Testing the correctness or incorrectness of this belief can be left to others. We have assumed it to be true here because it is easier to consider ideas and language separately rather than to lump them together into a single stage of the speech event.)

2. Grammatical encoding. Once speaker A has found the proper semantic units to express his thought, he must next arrange them in the particular way that his language requires. The scheme by which this arranging is done in a language is called the "grammar" of the language; we may therefore refer to this stage of the speech event as that of "grammatical encoding." For example, if A's language is English, and if he wants to get across the idea of "dog," "man," and "bite"—with the dog and not the man doing the biting—he has to encode it in the order *dog bites man;* the order *man bites dog* gives quite a different message. The grammatical code of Latin employs totally different devices. For the meaning "dog bites man" it marks the unit "dog" as a nominative (*canis*), the unit "man" as accusative (*virum*), and it can then combine these words with *mordet* 'bites' in any order whatever. For the opposite message it would mark "dog" as accusative (*canem*), "man" as nominative (*vir*), and it could then again combine these with *mordet* in any order at all. English grammar signals the difference between subject and object by means of word order; Latin grammar signals it by means of inflectional endings; other languages use still other devices.

The basic units used in grammatical encoding are called MOR-PHEMES (from Greek *morphḗ* 'form'). Morphemes may be either words: *dog, bite, man,* or parts of words: the *-s* of *bites*, the *-ing* of *biting*, etc. Some clearly correspond to semantic units: *dog, bite, man;* with others the semantic connection is less clear, e.g. *-s, -ing;*

still others seem to have no semantic connection at all, for example the *to* of *try to come* or the *-ly* of *quickly*. Morphemes are then arranged grammatically into such higher level units as WORDS: *bites, biting, quickly* (some morphemes are of course already words: *dog, bite, man, quick*); then PHRASES of various sorts, e.g. *the dog* (which can function, among other ways, as a "subject"), *bites the man* (a "predicate"); then CLAUSES of various sorts (in English, constructions containing a subject and predicate); and finally SENTENCES, which are marked in some way as not being parts of still larger constructions.

In the study of grammar it is useful to have a cover-term which will include grammatical units at all levels, from morpheme through word, phrase, clause, and sentence. For this the customary term is FORM. Examples of forms are: the morpheme and word *bite,* the morpheme (but not word) *-s,* the word (but not morpheme) *bites,* the phrase *bites me,* the clause *he bites me* . . . , and the sentence *He bites me.* It is also customary to make a rather sharp distinction between words on the one hand and larger forms on the other. The study of the way in which morphemes are grouped together to make words is called MORPHOLOGY; this deals with such forms as *bite-s, friend-ly, un-friend-ly, un-friend-li-ness,* or even that old favorite *anti-dis-establish-ment-ari-an-ism.* The study of the way in which words are grouped together to make phrases of various types is called SYNTAX; this deals with such forms as *the dog, bites me, the dog bites me* . . . , *The dog bites me,* etc.

The basic device of grammar is that of CONSTRUCTION: putting two (or more) forms together so as to give a larger form. Thus the two forms *friend* and *-ly* can be grouped together into the larger form (the "construction") *friendly;* the two forms *his* and *hat* can be grouped together into the construction *his hat;* etc. This disarmingly simple procedure is made infinitely productive by the fact that it can be applied over and over again, theoretically without end. That is to say, we can put a construction inside a construction inside a construction, and so on and on, like a Chinese puzzle. For example, we can put *friend* in construction with *-ly,* giving *friendly;* we can put this in construction with *un-,* giving *unfriendly;* and we can put this in construction with *-ness,* giving *unfriendliness.* Or: we can put *his* in construction with *hat,* giving *his hat;* we can put this in construction with *put on* (which is already a construction), giving *put on his hat;* and we can put this in construction with *the man* (which is already a construction), giving *the man put on his hat.*

This device of putting a construction inside a construction becomes, at least in theory, infinitely productive when we put a sentence (which is already a construction) inside another sentence; then put this inside still another sentence; and so on—a process known as EMBEDDING. For example, we can embed the sentence *Bill is coming* inside the sentence *John said (something),* giving *John said that Bill is coming;* we can embed this inside *Henry told George (something),* giving *Henry told George that John said that Bill is coming;* etc.

When a sentence is embedded within another sentence, it must undergo various types of TRANSFORMATION, depending on the grammatical function that it now fills. If *The dog bit the man* is embedded in "This is the dog," it appears as "This is the dog *that bit the man.*" Embedded in "I saw (something)," it appears as "I saw *the dog bite the man.*" Embedded in "I was horrified by (something)," it appears as "I was horrified by *the dog's biting the man.*" Embedded in "How was (something) possible?", it appears as "How was *it* possible *for the dog to bite the man?*" Every language has its own transformational rules for various types of embedding.

3. Phonological encoding. Once speaker A has given his message the proper grammatical encoding, he has—theoretically—a wide choice of means for transmitting it to B. Conceivably he could use any of the five senses, though probably only the senses of touch, sight, and hearing are sufficiently differentiated to allow for more than very simple communication. (One can at least imagine communication by taste or smell, but it would hardly get very far.) Should A now communicate tactilely by means of various degrees of softness, hardness, and contour? Or visually by means of various colors and shapes? Or auditorily by means of various sounds? Since we know that all human languages communicate by means of sound, it may seem ridiculous to consider these other possibilities; yet this naive approach to the medium of communication is precisely what we need if we want to take a fresh look at language and how it works.

Granted, then, that all human languages use sound as their medium of communication, what kind of sound do they use and how do they use it? If we wanted to be naive again, we could imagine human beings communicating with sound produced by clapping their hands, snapping their fingers, stamping their feet, etc. (After all, crickets communicate with sound produced by rubbing their hind legs together.) Human communication with this type of sound certainly occurs (nothing is sweeter to the ears of an actor than the sound of clapping hands); but human languages, in the usual sense of the term, universally use the type of sound that we call "speech," produced by various movements of the so-called "organs of speech": lungs, rib muscles, diaphragm, larynx, throat, nasal passage, palate, jaw, tongue, teeth, and lips. (Speech is of course not the primary function of any of these organs, any more than chirping is the primary function of a cricket's hind legs.) There are well documented reports of communication by means of other types of sound, such as "whistle speech" in Central America and the "drum languages" of Africa; but these other types all turn out to be clearly derived from ordinary speech and not to constitute an independent means of communication.

We have answered the question: "What kind of sound do human languages use?" But what of the question: "How do they use it?" We may recall that, as a result of grammatical encoding, the message at this point consists of a string of morphemes grouped at higher levels into words, phrases, clauses, and sentences. This string of morphemes now has to be converted into sound, i.e., it has to be phonologically encoded. The simplest method of doing this would be to convert each morpheme into a particular sound: one sound for *dog,* another for *bite,* another for *-s,* another for *man,* etc. If a language had only 30 or 40 morphemes, this would be a delightful method of encoding it phonologically: each basic grammatical unit (each morpheme) would then also be a phonological unit. But such a language would also have an impossible drawback: with only 30 or 40 morphemes one could not communicate very much—or could do so only by making each message monstrously long. In actual fact, every language has many thousands of morphemes, and a more ingenious method of phonological encoding has to be used. What every human language does is to encode its morphemes not into just *one* phonological unit each but into *one or more* phonological units each. These phonological units are called PHONEMES (from Greek *phōnḗ* 'sound'). For example, English encodes its morpheme *at* into two phonemes: /æt/, its morpheme *fish* into three: /fiš/, its morpheme *chest* into four: /čest/, its morpheme *thrift* into five: /θrift/, its morpheme *glimpse* into six: /glimps/, etc. By sheer chance some morphemes are encoded into only a single phoneme, e.g. the *-s* of *bites:* /-s/, or the *-ed* of *stopped:* /-t/; but this is not a necessary part of the system. (In order to distinguish phonemic symbols from phonetic symbols and from letters of the alphabet used in regular spelling, it is customary to write them between slant lines: / /. Just what particular phonemic symbols are used—e.g. /æ/ for the vowel of *at*, /š/ for the final consonant of *fish*, /č/ for the initial consonant of *chest*—is of no theoretical importance at all. If a language has, like English, more than 26 phonemes, one has to go beyond the 26 letters of the alphabet. In doing so, one tries as far as possible to choose symbols which are easy to write, type, and print.)

This device of encoding morphemes into sequences of phonemes, rather than into just one phonological unit each, is an extraordinarily powerful one. In terms of sheer economy, it is hard to overestimate its importance. If a language has 20 phonemes (a very modest number as the world's languages go) and allows itelf to encode only morphemes one phoneme in length, it can obviously have only 20 morphemes. But if the same language allows itself to encode morphemes which are 1, 2, 3, 4, and 5 phonemes in length (like English *a, at, cat, fast, blast*), the number of possible morphemes soon becomes astronomical. Theoretically (and we shall see in a moment that no language does just this), such a language could have the following number of morphemes:

1 phoneme in length	20	==	20
2 phonemes in length	20×20	==	400
3 phonemes in length	$20 \times 20 \times 20$	==	8,000
4 phonemes in length	$20 \times 20 \times 20 \times 20$	==	160,000
5 phonemes in length	$20 \times 20 \times 20 \times 20 \times 20$	==	3,200,000

Total number of morphemes $\overline{3,368,420}$

If the number of available phonemes is increased, the number of possible morphemes of course rises at a far faster rate. In a language with 30 phonemes (still allowing no more than 5 phonemes per morpheme) it is 25,137,930; and at 40 phonemes (English has between 30 and 40, depending on just how you figure them) it reaches the incredible total of 105,025,640.

We have given these figures to show what an enormous economy is achieved by having in human language this "duality principle," as it has been called: first an encoding into morphemes, and then a separate encoding of morphemes into one or more phonemes each. There is, however, a very bad flaw in our figures: we have assumed that it is possible for phonemes to occur in any mathematically possible sequence, such as (for English) /aaaaa/, /ppppp/, /fstgk/, etc. But English of course does not do this. Like every other language, it places strict limitations on the sequences of phonemes that can occur in a morpheme or in a word. For example, morphemes may begin (in English) with a vowel: *at,* or with one consonant: *rap,* or with two consonants: *trap,* or with three consonants: *strap,* but never with four or more. If a morpheme begins with three consonants, the first must be /s/, the second must be one of the set /p t k/, and the third must be one of the set /l r w y/; compare *split, strip, squint, spew.* Nevertheless, even with such strict limitations, the duality principle allows every language to form far more morphemes than it will ever use. If we take English to be a 30-phoneme language (it actually has more than 30, no matter how you figure them), allow no morphemes of more than 5 phonemes in length (*glimpse* has 6), and assume that only one out of every 1000 possible sequences of phonemes can be used, we still end up with a total of 25,137,930 divided by 1000 or 25,137 morphemes—enough to take care of any language. If we then remind ourselves that English words can easily consist of up to half a dozen morphemes, it is clear that we are also provided with an overabundance of possible word shapes.

If languages did their phonological encoding in the simplest possible manner, each morpheme at the grammatical level would be neatly matched by a corresponding morpheme at the phonological level, and each morpheme would always be encoded phonologically in the same way. Some languages live up to one or the other of these ideals—or almost; but many, including English, do not. At the grammatical level we can assume for English such morphemes as *horse, cat, dog, house, wife, bath, ox, child, man, woman, mouse,* etc., and also a morpheme "noun plural" which can be added to each of these. When we now look at the way English encodes these forms phonologically, we find the following:

Singular		Plural		Shape of morpheme "noun plural"
horse	/hórs/	horses	/hórsiz/	/-iz/
cat	/kǽt/	cats	/kǽts/	/-s/
dog	/dóg/	dogs	/dógz/	/-z/

house	/háus/	houses	/háuziz/	/-iz/
wife	/wáif/	wives	/wáivz/	/-z/
bath	/bǽθ/	baths	/bǽðz/	/-z/
ox	/áks/	oxen	/áksən/	/-ən/
child	/čáild/	children	/číldrən/	/-ən/
man	/mǽn/	men	/mén/	?
woman	/wúmən/	women	/wímin/	?
mouse	/máus/	mice	/máis/	?

The case of *horses, cats, dogs* (and others like them) is easily handled. All nouns of this type which end in sibilant or partially sibilant phonemes (/s z š ž č ǰ/) show the noun plural morpheme in the shape /-iz/: *horses, roses, bushes, garages, batches, badges;* all which end in other voiceless phonemes (/p t k f θ /) show the noun plural morpheme in the shape /-s/: *caps, cats, packs, cliffs, myths;* and all which end in other voiced phonemes (/b d g v ð m n ŋ l r/ and the vowels) show the noun plural morpheme in the shape /-z/: *ribs, beds, bags, caves, scythes, homes, cans, songs, sails, bears, seas, ways, spas, laws, foes, flues, pies, cows, boys, sofas.* These shapes of the noun plural morpheme are therefore PHONOLOGICALLY DETERMINED (i.e. determined by the phonological nature of the final phoneme of the noun), and they can be taken care of by three simple rules, namely: "Encode the morpheme 'noun plural' (1) after sibilants as /-iz/, (2) after other voiceless phonemes as /-s/, (3) after other voiced phonemes as /-z/." These are rules of great generality, and we will find that they also apply in other cases as well, for instance in the morpheme '3rd person singular present': /-iz/ in *he misses, he raises,* etc. (sibilants); /-s/ in *he stops, he hits,* etc. (voiceless); /-z/ in *he grabs, he bids,* etc. (voiced).

The forms *houses, wives, baths* (and many others like the latter two) require us to set up some special rules concerning the phonological encoding of the noun morphemes. Each of these must carry a tag reading: "Before adding noun plural morpheme, change final phoneme from voiceless to voiced." This will change /háus/ to /háuz-/, /wáif/ to /wáiv-/, /bǽθ/ to /bǽð-/. Once these changes have been made, we can apply the same rules as before to the noun plural morpheme: (1) /-iz/ after sibilant, giving /háuziz/; (3) /-z/ after other voiced phonemes, giving /wáivz/, /bǽðz/. The shapes of the noun plural morpheme are still phonologically determined.

When we come to *oxen* and *children,* however, we are required to set up a *special* rule for the phonological encoding of the noun plural morpheme. This must read: "After the morphemes *ox* and *child,* use shape /-ən/." (And *child* must carry a tag reading: "Before adding noun plural morpheme, change /čáild/ to /číldr-/.") Since in these rules we have to name the particular noun morphemes involved, the shape of the noun plural morpheme is not phonologically but MORPHOLOGICALLY DETERMINED. Nevertheless, it still has an identifiable shape, namely /-ən/.

The remaining three cases (to which we might add *feet, teeth,* etc.) require special rules of a different sort, since here we can no longer identify the shape of the noun plural morpheme. The rules themselves are simple enough: "Encode *man* + noun plural as /mén/; encode *woman* + noun plural as /wímin/; encode *mouse* + noun plural as /máis/; etc." But the implications of these rules are unfortunate: morphemes at the grammatical level are now no longer neatly matched by morphemes at the phonological level. The two grammatical units *"man"* and "noun plural" have been encoded as the single phonological unit /mén/; the two grammatical units *"woman"* and "noun plural" have been encoded as the single phonological unit /wímin/; and so on.

What lesson is there in this for the language learner? First, it is clear that he must learn those phonological encoding rules which have great generality, such as the conditions under which the noun plural morpheme has the shapes /-iz/, /-s/, and /-z/. Beyond that, he will do well to learn those encoding rules which apply to large numbers of forms, such as the rule that most English nouns ending in /-f/ and /-θ/ voice these to /-v/ and /-ð/ before adding the noun plural morpheme. As for the rest, we can offer him no solace. These are the familiar "irregular nouns," etc., of which we are all too aware, and they have to be learned as individual items. It is useful to look for as much regularity as possible in a language; but it is useless to look for regularity where it does not exist.

1, 2, 3. Semantic, grammatical, and phonological encoding. In the preceding sections we have assumed that a message is neatly encoded first semantically, then grammatically, and then phonologically. This is a useful fiction, because it allows us to consider each of these stages separately; but it is only a fiction. Normal speech is full of false starts, hesitations, grammatical irregularities, slips of the tongue, and the like. This means that we rarely plan a whole message carefully before we start sending it. Instead, we are a good deal more like the young lady who, when told that she should "think before she spoke," replied with rare honesty: "But I can't do that! How do I know what I'm going to say until I start talking?"

If we do not normally plan our entire message before we start sending it, we must possess some sort of feedback device which permits us to "monitor" the message as it is sent and to make necessary adjustments as we go along. In the case of semantic and grammatical encoding, we seem to have a storage device which keeps a record of what has just been sent so that later portions of the message can be referred back to it and encoded accordingly. Suppose we start out a sentence by saying: "If a driver comes to a stop street and doesn't actually make a full stop, . . ." If the monitoring is functioning properly, we can go on to say some such thing as: " . . . then he's liable to get arrested." If there is a slight slip in the grammatical encoding, it may end up as: ". . . then you'll get arrested." A slip in both semantic and grammatical encoding might produce something like: ". . . that's what happened to me." Only a complete breakdown in the monitoring system would lead to what could be called "nonsense," such as perhaps: " . . . it was two o'clock."

Though this type of semantic and grammatical monitoring must go on constantly, we know very little about it. Much better understood is "phonological monitoring," whereby a speaker hears the sounds of his own speech, decodes them phonologically, and is thus able to make sure that they never wander too far from the "phonological norms" that he seems to possess inside his head for each phoneme. He constantly hears his own speech not only via the vibrations which enter his ear from the air outside, but also via the vibrations of the bones near his ear (bone conduction). We can appreciate the importance of this constant phonological monitoring by considering the speech of persons who are unable to perform it, namely the deaf. If a person becomes totally deaf at, say, the age of twenty, for a while his speech may continue to sound quite natural. Kinesthetic monitoring of the movements of the speech organs apparently enables him to keep fairly close to the usual phonological norms. Gradually, however, his speech may wander farther and farther from the usual norms until it sounds "queer" to the normal hearer, and it may eventually become very difficult to understand or even quite incomprehensible.

4. From brain to speech organs. When phonological encoding has been completed, the message has been changed from a string of morphemes to a string of phonemes. Speaker A must now somehow program and send on down to his speech organs a set of instructions telling them what movements to make so as to turn each phoneme into sound. We can compare this with the way paper tapes are punched to provide instructions to automatic typewriters, telegraph transmitters, computers, and the like. Programmed in this way, the message is sent sequentially as electrochemical energy from the brain to the speech organs.

5. Movements of the speech organs. Triggered by successive innervations, the speech organs now perform the proper series of movements. As they do so, an interesting and rather disturbing thing becomes evident. We have assumed that when the message is sent on down to the speech organs, it is transmitted in the form of a sequence of separate instructions, one for each phoneme. If the message is the word *cat* /kæt/, for example, there would first be instructions for producing a /k/, then for producing an /æ/, and then for producing a /t/. If this assumption were correct, the speech organs would first assume the position for producing /k/, then move jerkily and instantaneously to the position for /æ/, and then move jerkily and instantaneously to the position for /t/. Commonsense tells us that the speech organs do not do this, and X-ray moving pictures of the speech organs in action prove it beyond a doubt. Instead of moving instantaneously to one position, holding it, and then moving instantaneously to another, the speech organs bobble back and forth in a constant flow of motion which does not seem to consist of any specific number of segments at all. A remarkable transformation has taken place: where the message previously consisted of a discrete number of segments—three, we assume, in the case of /kæt/—it has now been turned into a continuum. This transformation may seem relatively harmless at the moment, but it means that later on this continuum will have to be turned back into a series of discrete segments if the message is to be recovered. This is what must take place at Stage 9, "Phonological decoding."

Because of this slight fault in transmission, the separate phonemes of the phonological code are now represented by a string of sounds that overlap with one another. We can illustrate this by the following example. The phoneme /k/ in *keep* /kíp/, *cop*

/káp/, *coop* /kūp/ seems to us as speakers of English to be in each case the "same" /k/—as indeed it is in the built-in phonological code which we all possess as speakers of English. But if we listen carefully to the way our speech organs turn these /k/'s into audible sound, we will find them quite different from one another. This is easiest to hear if we start to say each of the three words *keep, cop, coop,* but then break the word off before we get to the vowel: *k-(eep), c-(op), c-(oop)*. When we hear the broken-off /k-/ of *k-(eep)*, we immediately know that it must be followed by the vowel *ee* /ī/, and similarly with the other two words. Indeed, if we ask a friend to pronounce a whole series of broken-off /k/'s, as in *k-(eep), c-(ape), c-(ap), c-(op), c-(aught), c-(ope), c-(oop)*, we can usually tell quite clearly what vowel would have followed if he had gone on to pronounce the whole word.

What causes this curious phenomenon? The answer seems to be that, by the time the speech organs have started to follow the instructions for producing /k/, they have also received most of the instructions for producing the following vowel. As a result, there is an overlapping of instructions which we can diagram as follows:

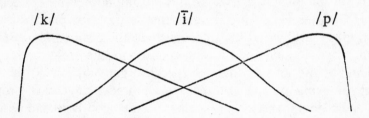

$$/k/ \qquad\qquad /\bar{\imath}/ \qquad\qquad /p/$$

How should we interpret this situation? Do we or don't we use the same *k* in *keep, cop, coop?* Phonetically—in terms of the sounds which our speech organs produce—there is no question but that we use a front [ḵ] before the front vowel of *keep,* a central [k] before the central vowel of *cop,* and a back [ḳ] before the back vowel of *coop.* We write these symbols in square brackets to show clearly that we are talking about PHONES (sound types) rather than PHONEMES. For phonemes are not sounds, but rather the abstract elements which exist somewhere inside our heads and which we use when we encode or decode phonologically.

This abstract nature of the phoneme is usually puzzling and even exasperating to those who are just becoming acquainted with the study of language. It often leads to some such question as:

"Well, do phonemes exist or don't they?" Alas, who knows! This is a little like asking whether a musical note exists. Is it one of the symbols which we see written in sheet music? No, that is just a way of symbolizing it on paper. Is it that bit of sound which a concert pianist has just played? No, not really; another pianist would have played it a little differently, perhaps slower or faster, or louder or softer. And the same note can also be played on a violin, a trombone, or a piccolo. Not that it will then *sound* the same; it won't. But it is still the "same note." It is an element in the structure of a musical composition; but you can't pick it up and look at it, or measure it, or even hear it. Does it exist? Who knows!

When a phoneme is realized phonetically by two or more different phones, these phones are said to be the ALLOPHONES of that phoneme. In the example just given the phones [ḵ], [k], [ḳ] (as well as a theoretically infinite number of intermediate phones) are allophones of the phoneme /k/. In this case, as we have suggested, the reason /k/ has these different allophones seems to be that the movements of the speech organs in producing the /k/ anticipate the movements which they are about to make to produce the following vowel. In the same way, the phoneme /æ/ shows different allophones in *bab, dad, gag* because of the different movements required in each case for the preceding and following /b/, /d/, /g/. This blending of sounds into one another—technically called "slur"—affects the phonetic realizations of all phonemes.

In the example just described, we have assumed that the phonological encoding of each of the /k/'s was identical, and that the allophonic differences arose because in the process of transmission the instructions for each /k/ were slurred into those of the following vowel. There seem to be other cases, however, where the encoding itself is responsible for allophonic differences. English *pie* and *spy* both contain the phoneme /p/, but it shows strikingly different allophones in the two words. In *pie* the /p/ is followed by strong "aspiration"—audible outflow of the breath stream; whereas in *spy* the /p/ has no such aspiration. Since this phonetic difference between the two /p/'s is not directly relevant to the phonological code of English, we have all had years of experience in overlooking it. The following experiment may help to make it clear. Light a match, hold it in front of your mouth, and say *spy* at it several times. The flame may flicker a bit, but it will hardly do more than that. Now hold the match in front of your mouth and say *pie* at it.

The aspiration of the /p/ will make the flame flicker strongly and probably even blow it out. The same experiment can also be performed with a thin slip of paper held in front of the mouth. The /p/ of *spy* will hardly cause it to move; the /p/ of *pie* will move it quite strongly.

How are we to explain this difference in the /p/'s of *pie* and *spy?* In *spy,* is there anything in the movements of the speech organs for the production of /s/ which would slur over into the following /p/ and stop it from being aspirated? This seems unlikely. If not, then the difference must lie farther back: the /p/ of *spy* must have been encoded differently from the /p/ of *pie.* Another example of this sort is such a word as *nun.* If this is recorded and then played backwards, it sounds like *nnnun,* with a very long /n/ at the beginning and a very short one at the end. This means that in normal order the initial /n/ is very short, the final /n/ much longer. Is slur somehow responsible for this? If not, then the two /n/'s must have been encoded differently.

When the speech organs interact in such a way as to produce a speech sound, they are said to ARTICULATE the sound. The study of this aspect of the speech event is accordingly called ARTICULATORY PHONETICS. A great deal of research has been done in this field, and there are many books which the language learner can read with great profit; a selection of them is listed in the Appendix. The reader is reminded again that all human beings have the same identical speech-producing apparatus. Different languages have different sounds not because their speakers have different speech organs but solely because they have in their heads different built-in (and learned!) phonological codes which send different instructions to the speech organs.

6. Vibrations of the air molecules. When speaker A sends a message from his brain, it exists momentarily in the form of electrochemical energy, as a sequence of slurred innervations. It is then turned into a continuum of mechanical energy in the form of movements of A's speech organs. These movements in turn produce a continuum of "sound"—vibrations of the air molecules. These vibrations fan out from A's mouth as "sound waves" and are available to hearer B or any other person close enough to receive the vibrations before they become inaudible.

The study of this aspect of the speech event is ACOUSTIC

PHONETICS. Here again a great deal of research has been done and some remarkable advances have been achieved especially since World War II. Though the field is a fascinating one, it offers little of direct use to the average language learner.

7. Vibrations of the ear. As the vibrations of the air molecules reach hearer B, they are transformed successively into a number of other types of vibratory energy in B's middle and inner ear. First they cause his eardrum to vibrate; these vibrations are then transmitted by further, corresponding vibrations of the three bones in the middle ear (hammer, anvil, stirrup); and these vibrations in turn cause corresponding vibrations of the cochlear fluid in the inner ear, where they seem to be picked up selectively by the hairs of the basilar membrane. It seems extraordinary that, beginning with the movements of A's speech organs and ending with the vibrations of the cochlear fluid in B's inner ear, the message can assume so many different forms and not be lost. Yet it *does* assume all these forms, and far more information is actually passed on to B's brain than he needs to use to recover the message.

The study of this aspect of the speech event has usually been combined with a study of the functioning of the ear in general. Though much has been learned, it has little or no application to ordinary language learning. A normal ear functions marvelously well; it is only farther along the line that a language learner gets into trouble.

8. From ear to brain. Though this stage is in a sense the mirror image of Stage 4, "From brain to speech organs," there are two important differences. First, before the message went from A's brain to his speech organs, it consisted of a string of discrete segments, one for each phoneme; but since in the process of transmission it was then turned into a "slurred continuum," this is the shape in which it now reaches B's brain. Second, speaker A was able to send the message only because, somewhere inside his head, he possessed the proper code; hearer B, however, can receive all the energy in the message whether he knows the code or not—though of course he can do nothing further with it unless he *does* know the same code. All of us can "hear" all there is to hear in any foreign-language message; we can "understand" the message only if we also know the foreign-language code.

9. Phonological decoding. In the speech event which we are considering, we assume that hearer B *does* possess inside his head the same phonological code as A. His task is therefore one of using this code to turn the "slurred continuum" of sound which he receives back into the same sequence of discrete phonemes that it had when speaker A sent it. We do not, of course, know how B really does this; but we can make some useful inferences from our own experience in decoding English.

Experience tells us that, when we listen to the speech of someone talking to us, we first of all shunt aside a good deal of the sound we hear as simply not belonging to the message. Not that it is necessarily "meaningless." It may contain a great deal of meaning, as we shall see in a moment; but we shunt it aside because it either does not belong to the language at all or does not belong to the language in the narrower sense of the term. First, what we hear may inform us about the speaker's physical condition: whether he has a cold (stuffed up nose, hoarse throat) or some physical disability (cleft palate, damaged vocal cords); what his age and sex are (child, man, woman, young or old); whether he is out of breath; and so on. Such things are presumably the same in all languages and hence not part of any code. Second, the sound we hear may allow us to identify the speaker (assuming that for some reason we cannot see him); this is at least in part because of the physical quality of his voice, and this again has nothing to do with the language.

Two further aspects of what we hear are highly conventional and definitely belong to "language," though they are not part of the "code" that we have been discussing thus far. First come those things which we often refer to as "it wasn't what he said but how he said it": things indicating that the speaker is angry, excited, sarcastic, unctuous, etc., and revealing his attitude toward himself, toward us, or toward the message. Since such matters are different in English from what they are in French or Vietnamese, they are clearly part of the English language in the wider sense of the term. (Study of these matters belongs to that fascinating branch of linguistics which has recently been dubbed "paralinguistics.") Finally, the type of semantic, grammatical, and phonological encoding which the speaker uses may tell us a great deal about where he comes from and what social and educational class he belongs to. The phonological encoding "thoity-thoid" will suggest that he comes from Brooklyn or thereabouts; the phonological encoding "thihty-thihd" will suggest that he comes perhaps from Boston. If he uses the grammatical encoding "I seen him when he done it," we will place him at a relatively low educational and social level—even though (and this is an interesting point) the message comes through just as clearly as if he had said "I saw him when he did it." (The study of these latter two aspects of language belongs to linguistic geography and sociolinguistics.)

When matters of this sort have been filtered out, we are left with that part of the sound that constitutes the actual message. We may recall that the sound reaches hearer B as a "slurred continuum." His task is now that of taking this continuum, matching it up with the phonological code which he has inside his head, and thereby breaking it up into the same sequence of discrete phonemes that the message had when it was sent to A's speech organs. This "breaking up" of the continuum of sound is necessary to regain the original message, and the compulsion to perform it is extraordinarily strong in all of us. Let us suppose, for example, that a friend introduces us to someone whom he calls "Mr. Maser," but that he pronounces the name with a sound which strikes us as halfway between /s/ and /z/. If it turns out that Mr. Maser's name is going to be important to us, we soon begin to fidget. Is the name /mésər/ (rhyming with *racer*) or /mézər/ (rhyming with *razor*)? It is odd that this should trouble us, since we already know perfectly well how to pronounce the name—namely with a sound halfway between /s/ and /z/. Yet it *does* trouble us, since such a halfway sound strikes us as somehow being "against the rules." And indeed it is. The rules of the phonological code of English do not allow for the possibility of a phoneme halfway between /s/ and /z/; they require that a name such as *Maser* be decoded either with an /s/ or with a /z/—a "halfway" phoneme is not admissible.

In our discussion of Stage 1, "Semantic encoding," we referred metaphorically to each language as "a vast sieve with thousands of semantic slots in it"; at the present stage of phonological decoding we can similarly think of each language as a sieve with (this time) a small number of "phonological slots." Any message that reaches us must be put through this sieve in such a way that every bit of sound (once we have shunted aside those aspects which do not belong strictly to the message) is assigned to one phoneme or another, with no halfway items.

The "slurred continuum" of ordinary speech is full of sounds that cannot be assigned to a specific phoneme on a purely phonological basis. Usually such items cause no trouble because we can refer the message farther up the line and get the answer there. For example, if our friend tells us that he is going over to the drugstore to buy a "raser," we can refer this part of the message on up to the semantic code and get the answer that this must be phonemically a /rézər/ razor and not a /résər/ racer, since the latter are not sold in drugstores. Personal names are instructive as examples precisely because no such referral to the semantic code is possible.

In worrying about Mr. Maser's name we are obeying one requirement of the phonological code: that the continuum of the message (as it reaches us) must be broken up into a sequence of English phonemes—with no "halfway phonemes" allowed. But there is also a second requirement: each phoneme sequence must be one that is permitted by the English phonological code. If we are introduced to someone whose name we at first decode as /tlǽnsī/, we will refuse to accept it this way. Though these are all perfectly good English phonemes, the English phonological code does not admit any words beginning with /tl-/. Maybe the name is Clancey, or Delancey; it just can't be "Tlancey."

10. Grammatical decoding. We assume at this stage that the message, neatly broken up into a sequence of phonemes, is being passed along from the phonological to the grammatical code. Hearer B's task is now one of grouping these phonemes into grammatical units of various sizes: morphemes, words, phrases, clauses, sentences—as well as larger structures involving sequences of sentences. Somehow he must take the message as it arrives, match it against his own built-in grammatical code (which must be essentially the same as A's), and decode it in this way. How does he do it? Of course, we do not really know; but we can make some pretty shrewd guesses.

Most of us usually think of decoding as being done largely in terms of meaning—that is, by referring everything directly to the semantic code. We surely do a great deal of this; but we can also do a great deal of decoding on a purely grammatical basis, without reference to the semantic code at all. As proof of this, consider the following famous bit of English, from Lewis Carroll's *Jabberwocky:*

'Twas brillig, and the slithy toves
Did gyre and gimble in the wabe;

> All mimsy were the borogoves,
> And the mome raths outgrabe.

Here we can make almost no appeal to the semantic code, since all the CONTENT WORDS (words strong in semantic reference) have been replaced by nonsense forms; the only words left are the FUNCTION WORDS, which serve primarily to indicate grammatical structure. But since they *do* indicate grammatical structure, we will find that if we match this bit of "English" against our built-in grammatical code, we can decode the entire grammatical meaning.

Because *brillig* fills the slot X in "it was X," our grammatical code tells us that it must be either a noun (" 'twas evening") or an adjective (" 'twas sultry"). Both of these constructions ("it was NOUN," "it was ADJECTIVE") are common English clause types. Next, the word *the* signals the fact that, before long, a noun is going to follow; presumably it is the word *toves*. There are two clues to support this assumption. First, the *-s* of *toves* seems to be the noun plural suffix we have already talked about (and here, following /v/, it must have the shape /-z/: /tóvz/). Second, the *-y* of *slithy* is a common suffix which derives adjectives from nouns (compare *slime, slimy*), and this would give the very common noun phrase type "the ADJECTIVE NOUN." Of course, *toves* could also be a verb (with the same *-s* as *moves* or *loves*); but this is unlikely, since it is immediately *followed* by a verb, namely *did*. The evidence is therefore overwhelmingly in favor of decoding *the slithy toves* as "the ADJECTIVE NOUN-s"; and, because this noun phrase occurs in first position in the clause, it must be the subject of the following verb *did*. (The example *Dog bites man* has already alerted us to the use of word order as a clue to the subject of an English sentence.) The word *did*, followed by *gyre and gimble*, is ambiguous: it may be a full verb, in which case *gyre* and *gimble* are its objects (parallel to "did algebra and geometry"); more likely it is an auxiliary verb, and the full verbs are *gyre* and *gimble* (parallel to "did dance and gambol"). Whichever solution we choose, it is clear that *gyre* and *gimble* are the same part of speech (either both nouns or both verbs), since we know that *and* always connects identical forms. Continuing, the word *in* signals with almost complete certainty that a noun will soon follow; and the following word *the* signals the same thing, now with even greater certainty. Hence *wabe* simply *must* be a noun, and the whole construction is a typical prepositional phrase: "in the NOUN." Now we know the grammatical structure of the second clause: it consists of a noun phrase as subject (*the slithy toves*), plus a predicate made up of an auxiliary verb with two coordinate full verbs (*did gyre and gimble*) followed by an adverbial prepositional phrase (*in the wabe*). We "know" all these things because we possess them in our built-in English grammatical code.

Is it really true that we go through some such process as this every time we decode a message grammatically? To this the answer seems to be: Yes, it is really true. Or, perhaps more realistically: It *seems* to be true; if anybody has a better theory, let him present it. We need not worry about the amount of time involved. The grammatical code is built in so firmly that our brain can perform the above matchings almost instantaneously. And in actual decoding we do not verbalize all our various matchings, as we have above; they are performed in a flash. Furthermore, in normal decoding we gain speed by matching things up with the semantic code. That is why we can decode such a sentence as " 'Twas evening, and the lively elves did dance and gambol in the glade" a good deal faster than we can decode the first four lines of *Jabberwocky*.

Sometimes our grammatical decoding leads to ambiguous results. How, for example, should we decode such a sentence as: *The shooting of the soldiers is deplorable?* Here *the shooting of the soldiers* can be interpreted either as a transformation of "The soldiers shoot (but the way they do so is deplorable)," or as a transformation of "Someone shoots the soldiers (and this is deplorable)." Since both transformations have the same shape (*the shooting of the soldiers*), the sentence is grammatically ambiguous. We can only hope that this ambiguity will be resolved when we consult the semantic code.

11. Semantic decoding. Here we can be brief—because we know so little. Insofar as speaker A and hearer B share the same semantic code, there is no problem. However, this is the part of the total code which differs the most from speaker to speaker. It seems that no two speakers share the exact same semantic code, and sometimes the differences within a given language can be very great. If, in a political discussion, you describe someone as a "liberal," you may put a positive value on this term whereas I put a negative value on it—or vice versa. Differences of this sort can be very troublesome precisely because we do not realize that they exist. Minor differences from person to person in the phonological and grammatical codes are quite obvious, and we are easily able to adjust to them. But similar minor differences in the semantic code often go undetected and hence cause major misunderstandings.

9, 10, 11. Phonological, grammatical, and semantic decoding. We have again treated three stages in the speech event as if they belonged in distinct compartments and were neatly separated from one another. But this time, even more than before, all three stages must be considered together. Probably all of us have had the experience of listening to a speaker, being puzzled by something he said, and not figuring it out until he was halfway through the next sentence. How do we do this? Two things seem clear. First, we must have a powerful storage device which allows us to preserve the first sentence for examination and at the same time to receive the next sentence as it reaches us. (This storage device has limits, of course. We very often miss the second sentence precisely because in the meantime we have been trying to figure out the first one.) Second, as we are examining the first sentence, it seems likely that we scan it in all possible ways. Since it didn't go through properly the first time, we re-check it phonologically, we re-check it grammatically, and we re-check it semantically. Eventually we do—or don't—hit upon an interpretation which "makes sense."

Suppose, for example, we receive a message which we tentatively decode as: "I'll senate by air mail. Then he'll be sure . . ." At the phonological level this causes no trouble: /sénit/ is a perfectly acceptable sequence of phonemes. At the grammatical level there is at first no difficulty; we even find there a lexical item of this shape, namely *senate*. But then we begin to run into trouble. The item *senate* is marked as "noun," whereas the code tells us that, in "I'll X by Y," the X must be a verb. Still, the grammatical code also tells us that most simple nouns can be used as verbs (compare "to *table* a motion," "to *chair* the meeting," etc.). A quick check in the semantic code, however, reveals that "to senate by air mail" just doesn't make sense. So back we go again to the phonological code. Here, stored off in a corner somewhere, we find the further information that lots of speakers of American English drop final /d/ after /n/, as in /fáin/ for /fáind/ *find*, /sáun/ for /sáund/ *sound*, and—here we have it—/sén/ for /sénd/ *send*. So we try replacing /sénit/ with /séndit/ and then putting *this* through the system. It passes the phonological code, since this is an acceptable sequence of phonemes. It passes the grammatical code, since here there is an item marked "*send,* verb transitive" (i.e., it can take an object, such as *it*). And it passes the semantic code, since this tells us that one does indeed "send" things by air mail. All of this has happened in a flash. By this time the speaker is saying ". . . be sure . . . ," but the storage device has preserved the "Then he'll . . ." for us, so that we are able to get all of the next sentence.

We are vaguely conscious of this constant scanning—racing back and forth from one part of the total code to the other—only when we get temporarily stuck, as in "I'll senate by air mail" or, to give another example, "I hope this will suture plans." Apparently, however, we do just this sort of scanning all the time. We do not first decode phonologically, then grammatically, then semantically, but rather do all three more or less at once. There is good experimental evidence to prove that we do not decode phonemes solely on the basis of the sound stimuli which reach us. We also use clues from the rules concerning possible sequences of phonemes (e.g., rejecting an initial /tl-/ and replacing it by /kl-/), from the rules of the grammatical code, from our built-in store of known morpheme and word shapes, and from the rules of the semantic code.

To help us in our decoding we also use clues from *outside* of language, namely from the situation in which the utterance occurs. Suppose, for example, that someone says to me: "Take the big one upstairs." This is grammatically ambiguous, since it can be either (1) "The big one upstairs is to be taken," or (2) "The big one is to be taken upstairs." But let us assume that the sentence occurs in a situation when my family is moving to our summer house and I am dutifully loading things into the station wagon. Having been told to take along a lamp, I choose the little one in the study and am about to put it into the car. If my wife then says to me: "Take the big one upstairs," the situation tells me that this must be the equivalent of grammatical structure (1). Suppose, however, that we have arrived at the summer house, that I am unpacking the car, and that I walk in the door with two lamps in my hands, a big one and a little one. If my wife then says to me: "Take the big one upstairs," the situation tells me that this must be the equivalent of grammatical structure (2).

A very important role in the decoding of speech is played by what is technically called REDUNDANCY. Stated very briefly, redundancy is the difference between the amount of information a code or a message theoretically *could* carry and the amount of information it actually *does* carry. Written numbers have no redundancy at all. If I write a check for $367 and one of the numbers is illegible, the bank will not know how much money to pay. That is why they also ask me to write the number out in letters, where the redundancy is very high: even if several of the letters are illegible, the message still comes through. Speech also has high redundancy—usually estimated at something like 50%. In speech, the message "I do not want to go" is ideally /ái dū nát wónt tū gó/. But here there is so much redundancy that it can be reduced to /áidə wónə gó/ ("Ida wanna go") and still be perfectly intelligible.

Redundancy is something which every foreign language learner will run into in situations like the following. Suppose you are sitting in a noisy restaurant in Paris with a group of French friends, each of whom you know well. Despite the clatter of plates and the buzz of conversation from other tables, *they* are able to communicate with no difficulty at all; whereas *you*, the foreigner, are hardly able to understand a word they are saying. This is infuriating, since you know that you can understand each of them perfectly when the two of you are alone in a quiet room. Why can't you understand them now? The answer is redundancy. Just as you are able to reconstruct from the mangled *Ida wanna go* the full message *I do not want to go,* so they are able to reconstruct full messages from the distorted sound they hear through the clatter of dishes and the buzz of conversation. You, however, do not yet know the code well enough to do this. With time and practice you will; but this particular job takes a *lot* of time and practice. Redundancy explains why we are all horrified at the thought of having to telephone in a foreign language, or why we understand the sound track of a foreign film far less well than we understand a live speaker. In both cases a good deal of the sound has not been transmitted to us. A native knows the total code well enough so that he can reconstruct the full message from this incomplete transmission. We, as foreign learners, still do not know the total code that well.

Chapter Four

Sounds

How does one learn to produce and understand the sounds of a foreign language? If we were children, we could do so simply by imitation and mimicry: listening to the way others talk, and then making exactly the same sounds in exactly the same way. Though a few adults are able to do this almost as well as children, most of us cannot. We make the mistake of using our English phonological code, so that we tend to produce the foreign language sounds as if they were English sounds, and even to hear them as if they were English sounds. Though it is true that most of us suffer badly from this error, it is also true that we suffer far more than we need to. If we honestly try to imitate the foreign sounds as we hear them—no matter how ridiculous they seem to us—most of us can do a very good job of imitation. What holds us back is largely the "foreignness" of the sounds—precisely the fact that they are different from those of English. Overcoming this inability is not a physiological matter (since we possess all the sound-producing equipment that is needed) but rather a psychological one. To get ourselves into the proper frame of mind, what we need to do is to pretend that we are making a hilariously funny imitation of the foreign speaker—imitating every sound, every tone of voice, every mannerism, even every gesture. We hesitate to do this, of course, because—being polite—we are afraid the foreigner will think that we are making fun of him. But anyone who has ever tried such wholehearted imitation will know that the results are just the opposite. The foreign speaker's eyes will light up with pleasure, he will tell us that now, at last, we are saying things the right way, and he will even be flattered by the thought that he is such a good "teacher."

If the foreign teacher speaks English poorly, there is another kind of "imitation" which we can use—though this time it is better not to use it in his presence. If his pronunication of English is miserable, this is because he is making just the kinds of errors we do, but in reverse: he is encoding the sounds according to the phonological code of *his* language, and not according to that of *ours*. So much the better for us! We can attempt to make a hilariously funny imitation of the way he speaks English, and thus use a second device to get at the phonological encoding processes of his language. Anyone who can imitate a thick Swedish accent in English can also speak *Swedish* with a thick Swedish accent—which is precisely the way the Swedes speak it. Many people have marvelous imitative abilities of this sort. It is curious that they so often drop them as soon as they start to learn a foreign language, since this is the one place they can really make good use of them.

These two ways of learning a foreign pronunciation strike most adults as somehow "unintellectual" and hence not desirable in the serious business of foreign language learning. This is a shame, since both methods are highly effective. Perhaps it is too much to ask a learner to make fun of his teacher's pronunciation of English, since this seems so impolite. Imitating the teacher's pronunciation of his *own* language, however, is not impolite at all; indeed, it is a compliment of the highest sort and will produce reactions of pleasure and gratitude. If the learner will only "let himself go" and indulge in a little harmless theatrics, he can attain excellent results without recourse to the "intellectual" devices which we are about to describe.

What are these "intellectual" devices? One of them is the study of phonetics. Any adult can profit greatly from reading a book on general phonetics, which will tell him what kinds of sounds are used in the languages of the world and what types of movements of the speech organs are used to produce them. Such books are never a substitute for direct imitation, but they may make imitation a good deal easier because it can then be understood intellectually. Very good also are those books which deal with the phonetics of a particular language, especially if they contrast it with the phonetics of English. Because a full discussion of phonetics would go far beyond the bounds of this book, we shall not attempt it here. A number of excellent treatments of phonetics are listed in the Appendix.

Another way of learning foreign language sounds "intellectually" is to recall what was said in the preceding chapter about phonological encoding. The basic elements in the phonological code of any language are the phonemes; and the fundamental fact about any phoneme is that it is realized in sound differently from any other phoneme. Theoretically, at least (though this is not entirely true in practice), we can pronounce a phoneme any way we want to just as long as it does not get in the way of the sounds used for other phonemes. In many languages, for example, there is a phoneme /r/ which is pronounced in either of two quite different ways: either by bringing the tongue-tip against the gum ridge behind the upper teeth (a "tongue-tip /r/"), or else by raising the back of the tongue up against the uvula (a "uvular /r/"). Some speakers of French, German, Dutch, Indonesian, etc. use one kind of /r/, some use the other, some use both. As long as these pronunciations do not overlap with those of other phonemes, the essential nature of the phonological code remains intact. The fundamental nature of a phoneme is its "otherness"—the fact that it sounds different from every other phoneme in the language.

If we apply this basic fact of language structure to the problem of language learning, it is clear that a learner's first task is to be able to pronounce all the phonemes of the foreign language in such a way as to keep them distinct from one another. A foreigner learning English may find it difficult (because of the bias of his native language phonological code) to hear and produce the difference between the vowels of *beat* and *bit, feet* and *fit, heat* and *hit,* tending to use an intermediate sound for both of them. Or he may find it difficult to make the difference between the initial consonants of *sin* and *thin, sank* and *thank, sought* and *thought,* tending to pronounce them both as *s.* And yet, difficult or not, such distinctions simply *must* be learned if a very fundamental aspect of the English language is not to be destroyed. Similarly, if we as speakers of English are learning French, we simply *must* learn to hear and produce the difference between the two vowels often written phonemically as /i/ and /y/: *vie* and *vu* (/vi/, /vy/), *lit* and *lu* (/li/, /ly/); or between the plain and nasalized vowels of such pairs of words as *bas* and *banc* (/ba/, /bã/), *cas* and *quand* (/ka/, /kã/).

How can we learn such things? The first and most obvious step is to make sure that we can accurately *hear* such differences; until we have learned to, there is not even a chance of our being able to *pronounce* them. So we begin by having the foreign speaker say precisely such pairs as *vie* vs. *vu, lit* vs. *lu,* or *bas* vs. *banc, cas* vs. *quand,* until we catch on to the differences. Then we ourselves try to *produce* these same differences, imitating the foreign speaker and using him to guide and correct us. The chances are that he will not be fully satisfied with our pronunciations, but as a first step it is enough if he can tell which member of the pair we are trying to say—whether it is *vie* or *vu, lit* or *lu.* If we can once get this far, we will have satisfied the minimal requirement of keeping the phonemes of the foreign language apart. Communication in the foreign language will then be possible, though not necessarily elegant.

The next step is to try to put a little polish on our minimally acceptable pronunciations. We not only want to pronounce the /i/ and /y/ of *vie* and *vu* differently; we also want to pronounce each of them as nearly as possible in the way a Frenchman does. Though mimicry and a knowledge of phonetics are our best weapons, there is one further device which can be helpful. To the extent that we are pronouncing the /i/ of French *vie* etc. in the wrong way, we are almost certainly doing so because we are pronouncing it like the nearest equivalent vowel of English, in this case the vowel of *Vee, see, me, he,* etc. How shall we learn the difference between the two? Again, we start out by learning to *hear* it. Using a tape recorder, we record first our teacher's pronunciation of French *vie,* then our own pronunciation of English *Vee;* next, our teacher's pronunciation of French *si,* then our own pronunciation of English *see;* etc. If we now listen to this tape recording, we can grasp the difference between these French and English vowels that seem so much alike to us. We then go on to make another, similar recording; only this time, instead of pronouncing our normal vowel of *Vee* etc., we try our best to use the proper French sound—mimicking as hard as we can and trying to make use of the differences which the preceding recording showed us. We then play back this recording and see how well we have done.

Once we think we have most of the phonemes of the foreign language more or less under control—both phonemically (in terms of keeping them apart from one another) and phonetically (in terms of making them sound right)—we can make good use of another type of recording. Here we listen to short phrases and sentences in the foreign language, concentrating first on one aspect of them (e.g. some vowels which have caused us trouble), then on another aspect (e.g. some consonants or consonant combinations which have caused us trouble). In particular, at this point we also pay special attention to such matters as timing, rhythm, and intonation. (These are things which a learner is likely to overlook, yet they are among the most important of all in making one's pronunciation "sound right.") Next, we play the same phrases and sentences over again and try to imitate them as accurately as possible—concentrating entirely on their sound rather than, as one usually does, on their meaning. If we have the recording equipment to do so, we can even record our imitations right after the original foreign language version and then play back this combined recording to see how well we have done. We will not consciously "hear" all our faulty pronunciations, but with a little concentration we can hear—and hence be able to correct—a great many of them.

When we talk with someone in our native language, we know the phonological code so thoroughly that we can afford to concentrate entirely on *what* the person is saying rather than on *how* he is saying it. In learning a foreign language, our ultimate goal is of course the ability to handle it in just this same way. However, we cannot reach this goal until we have acquired a comparable mastery of the foreign language's phonological code; and to gain this mastery we need to spend a good part of our learning time concentrating on *how* a foreign speaker says things, even if this means temporarily neglecting *what* he is saying. Be sure you reserve a good proportion of your learning time for this purpose. It is extraordinary how many language learners neglect this important and obvious step in the total language learning process.

In the above discussion we have several times mentioned the fact that most of our mispronunciations occur because we tend to use in the foreign language the phonological code of our native English—just as our teacher's mispronunciations (assuming they are miserable) come from the fact that *he* tends to use in English the phonological code of *his* native language. In order to help ourselves avoid mistakes of this sort, we need to consider some of the features of American English pronunciation which are not likely to occur in a foreign language, since it is precisely these things which we must avoid. And we must of course also consider those features *lacking* in English which we are likely to encounter in a foreign language—though we can mention this topic only briefly, since a full coverage of it can be given only in a book on general phonetics.

Unfamiliar sounds. The inexperienced language learner usually thinks that he is going to have the greatest trouble in learning to pronounce totally unfamiliar sounds in the foreign language, such as the vowel of French *vu* 'seen' or *pu* 'been able,' or the final consonant of German *Bach* 'brook' or *Loch* 'hole.' There is no question but that such sounds do cause difficulty. On the other hand, precisely because they *are* unfamiliar, the learner immediately recognizes them as a problem. Learning them is then only a matter of imitation (aided by a phonetic knowledge of how they are produced) plus, above all, practice and persistence.

Familiar sounds. A far greater learning problem is presented by those sounds which seem similar to what we have in English, because the learner is then likely to substitute the corresponding English sounds and never even realize that a learning problem exists. An excellent example is the American English /r/. As the languages of the world go, this is a rare sound, and it is highly unlikely that the learner will encounter it in any foreign language he learns. Our American English /r/ is produced by a peculiar constriction of the tongue, while at the same time the tongue-tip is often arched up toward the middle of the roof of the mouth. If the foreign language we are learning has an /r/-like phoneme at all, it is far more likely to be produced by a quick flip of the tongue-tip against the gum ridge above the upper teeth (a "flapped" /r/, much like a common pronunciation of American /t/ in *city*), or by two or three vibrations of the tongue-tip against gum ridge (a "trilled" /r/, such as children often use in imitating a telephone bell or a policeman's whistle); or it may be a kind of gargling sound, produced by raising the back of the tongue against the back of the roof of the mouth and the uvula (a "uvular" /r/), sometimes accompanied by a few vibrations of the uvula (a "trilled" uvular /r/). The learner should listen hard to find out just what kind of /r/ is used in the foreign language he is learning, and then imitate it as closely as he can. He should, above all, *not* be so foolish as to succumb to the temptation to use our American /r/ instead. Probably nothing contributes more to a horrible American accent than the naive use of our familiar constricted /r/ in a foreign language.

Another example, which can be almost as offensive in many foreign languages, is the American English /l/. This is typically produced by putting the tongue-tip against the gum ridge and, at the same time, raising the back of the tongue toward the roof of the mouth. It is this raising of the back of the tongue which gives to our /l/ its characteristic hollow sound. Though this so-called "dark /l/" also occurs in a good many other languages (Dutch, for example), the learner is more likely to find that the language he is learning (if it has an /l/-like phoneme at all) uses a "clear /l/," produced *without* any raising of the back of the tongue. To us, this sounds like pretty much the same thing as our dark /l/ and we therefore tend to overlook the difference. However, using our dark /l/ produces a rather unpleasant effect in many foreign languages, and the learner should, then, avoid it.

American English /b d g/ (as in *buy, die, go*) and /p t k/ (as in *pie, tie, cow*) differ from one another in that /b d g/ are VOICED (pronounced with simultaneous vibrations of the vocal cords) whereas /p t k/ are VOICELESS (pronounced without vibrations of the vocal cords). In addition, the difference between the two sets is reinforced by the fact that /p t k/ are aspirated in certain positions (e.g. word-initially in *pie, tie, cow*, though not after /s/ in *spy, sty, scow*); and, perhaps as a result of this reinforcement, the voicing of /b d g/ is often very weak. (We can afford to voice /b d g/ very weakly, since lack of aspiration still distinguishes them in most positions from /p t k/.) Some foreign languages—German, for example—handle /b d g/ and /p t k/ in much this same way. More commonly, however, languages which have all six of these phonemes *never* aspirate /p t k/; and, perhaps for this reason (so that there will be no confusion between the two sets), they tend to voice /b d g/ more fully than we do in English. These are subtle differences; but if the learner will look for them and imitate them, he will greatly improve his foreign language pronunciation. These are some of the things which, in reverse, make Russians (or Frenchmen, or Italians) sound so funny to *us*.

American English /t/ and /d/ are pronounced in most positions by putting the tongue-tip against the gum ridge above the upper teeth; note, for example, that this is (almost surely) the way you pronounce them in such words as *to, do,* or *at, add*. But in one special position, namely before /θ/, most of us pronounce them by putting the tongue-tip against the upper teeth; see if you do not do this in such words as /ḗtθ/ *eighth* and /wídθ/ *width*. (This is an example of "slur": the instructions to the speech organs tell them to articulate /θ/ by forcing air through a narrow slit between the tongue-tip and the upper teeth, not the gum-ridge; these instructions are then anticipated in the articulation of the preceding /t/ or /d/ in *eighth, width,* etc.) In many languages—for example, Italian—the corresponding phonemes /t/ and /d/ are *always* produced by putting the tongue-tip against the upper teeth, and not against the gum ridge. Though this may seem like a very minor difference, using a "dental" /t/ and /d/ will make your Italian sound that much better.

When American English /t/ stands between a stressed vowel and an unstressed vowel (as in *latter, writing*), many of us use a special allophone which makes *latter* sound almost like *ladder, writing* sound almost like *riding,* etc. Carrying this habit over into a foreign language should be avoided (unless the foreign language does the same thing, which is most unlikely). It will cause confusion particularly in those languages which use a flapped tongue-tip /r/, since this latter and our special /t/ allophone sound almost the same.

American English has an interesting vowel system in which many vowels tend more or less strongly to be pronounced as diphthongs—that is, not as "steady state" vowels with a single vowel quality held throughout, but as glides from one vowel position toward another. This is particularly true of the vowels /ē/ and /ō/ (as in *say, dough*), somewhat less true of the vowels /ī/ and /ū/ (as in *see, do*). More likely than not, such diphthongal pronunciations will sound very queer in the foreign language you are learning. Listen hard to hear whether the corresponding foreign language vowels (assuming there are such) are diphthongized or not. Probably they will not be. From years of practice with English you will have a strong temptation to diphthongize all vowels of this type. Resist this temptation.

Splitting an English phoneme. A problem which the learner may at first not even realize exists can occur when two sounds which function as allophones in English correspond to two sounds which function as different phonemes in the foreign language. We have mentioned several times that aspirated [pʰ tʰ kʰ] occur in some positions in English, for example word-initially in *pie, tie, cow;* and that unaspirated [p t k] occur in some other positions, for example after /s/ in *spy, sty, scow.* Since these two different types of sounds never contrast with one another in any given position, we look upon them as simply different varieties of the same thing (technically, as allophones of one phoneme each). Indeed, we have had so many years of practice in *disregarding* the difference between aspirated and unaspirated that it often takes considerable listening practice before we can even convince ourselves that such a difference really exists. We therefore face a serious problem when we start to learn a language (such as Hindi) in which these are not allophones of a single phoneme each, but rather constitute independent and contrasting phonemes: /pʰ tʰ kʰ/ vs. /p t k/. Now we are required to split our phonemes right down the middle, as it were: to use both /pʰ/ and /p/ in word-initial position, to use both of them also after /s/, and so on. However, the difficulty is not as great as it may at first seem, since we already know how to pronounce both types of sounds (aspirated and unaspirated). The greatest difficulty is understanding that a problem exists in the first place.

Combining two English phonemes. In the preceding example, two allophones of English correspond to two different phonemes in the foreign language. We can also have the opposite situation: two phonemes of English which correspond to a single phoneme in the foreign language. In English we make a clear phonemic contrast between /d/ (as in /dén/ *den,* /lṓd/ *load*) and /ð/ (as in /ðén/ *then,* /lṓð/ *loathe*). In Spanish much the same two sounds exist, but they function as allophones of a single phoneme—spelled with the letter *d.* After pause, /n/, or /l/ this is pronounced as [d] (though it is a dental sound rather than a gum-ridge sound like our /d/): *dama* 'lady', *mundo* 'world', *caldo* 'broth'; but after a vowel it is pronounced as [ð]: *la dama* 'the lady', *modo* 'way', *cada* 'each'. Since both sound types are familiar to us, this presents no great learning problem. We need to remember, however, that a word such as *dama* will be pronounced with either [d] or [ð], depending on what precedes it.

A more serious learning problem occurs where two English

phonemes correspond to one foreign language phoneme, but the one foreign language phoneme sounds rather different from either of ours. For example, English has two phonemes of the type generally called "liquid": /l/ and /r/, as in *led* vs. *red, mirror* vs. *miller, eel* vs. *ear.* Japanese, however, has only one liquid phoneme; it is customarily transcribed /r/, though it could just as well be transcribed /l/. To us, it seems perversely to sound more like /r/ in some positions, more like /l/ in others. In fact, of course, it is neither /r/ *nor* /l/, but rather the one Japanese phoneme of this general phonetic type. To learn it, we must first disabuse ourselves of the idea that it ought to be either /r/ *or* /l/ and accept its midway position. Then we can get on with the job of imitating it as exactly as possible.

Using an English "non-phoneme." In English we commonly use a glottal stop (symbolized [ʔ]) in such forms as [ʔ]*uh*-[ʔ]*uh* meaning 'no', and also in careful pronunciations of such phrases as *not* [ʔ]*at* [ʔ]*all* when we want to avoid running these words together as *nota-tall.* For us this is not a phoneme; we look on it as a sort of catch in the throat which we can use in front of any word beginning with a vowel. In a great many languages, however, this same sound constitutes a phoneme /ʔ/, and it is just as much of a consonant as are /p/, /t/, or /k/. The only real learning problem involved here is that of realizing that it *is* a phoneme like other phonemes, and not just a device for separating vowels from what precedes. We already know how to make the sound; we merely have to learn that it can function in a new way, different from that of English.

Consonant clusters. Though we have large numbers of consonant clusters in English, we also place very strict limitations on what clusters can occur in what positions. For example, though we can freely use such word-initial clusters as /dr-/ (*dry, drink*), /kl-/ (*clip, claw*), and /sn-/ (*snap, snow*), we find it almost inconceivable that words should be able to begin with such other clusters as /dv-/, /kt-/, or /mn-/. And yet precisely such clusters occur freely in, for example, Russian: *dvá* 'two', *któ* 'who', *mnógo* 'much'. Because these clusters violate our English "cluster rules," we tend to insert our favorite unstressed vowel (that in the first syllables of *devote, catarrh, menagerie*) between the two consonants and to say such things as [dəvá], [kətó], and [mənógə]. But if we listen carefully, we will notice that Russian speakers do *not* use this inserted vowel. These are real consonant clusters; and, insofar as they contain only sound types familiar to us, they do not constitute a serious learning problem. But we must be on the alert for them, and avoid imposing our English habits upon them.

Distributional problems. In English we find it only natural that /h/ should occur at the beginning of words or parts of words (*head, ahead*), though never at the end; and that /ŋ/ should occur at the middle or at the end of words (*singer, sing*), though never at the beginning. But this is "natural" only for English (plus those other languages which happen to share this peculiarity), and not for languages in general. There are many languages in which /h/ can occur at the end of a word, and many languages in which /ŋ/ can occur at the beginning. Once one accepts this fact, there is no great learning problem, since we already know how to make both sounds. We merely have to learn to use them in new positions.

A more serious distributional problem results from the way we handle unstressed vowels in English; and the worst of it is that most of us are quite unaware of what we do. In a word like *able* we use the vowels /ē/ and /ə/: /ébəl/; but in *ability* these shift to /ə/ and /i/: /əbílitī/. In a word like *atom* we use /æ/ and /ə/: /ǽtəm/; but in *atomic* these shift to /ə/ and /a/: /ətámik/. And in a word like *prophet* we use /a/ and /i/: /práfit/; but in *prophetic* these shift to /ə/ and /e/: /prəfétik/ (or, for some speakers, to /ō/ and /e/: /prōfétik/). Though we have a vowel /ā/, as in /fáðər/ *father*, it never occurs unstressed at the end of a word: despite its spelling, a word such as *sofa* is pronounced /sófə/ and not /sófā/. In short, we have a very complex system of handling vowels in unstressed syllables, and there are many types of unstressed syllables in which the only vowels that normally occur are /i/ (as in the second syllable of *service*) or /ə/ (as in the second syllable of *nervous*). As a result, we find it very difficult to pronounce other vowels in such positions, and we tend to render all sorts of unstressed foreign language vowels as either /i/ or /ə/. There are, of course, foreign languages which also handle *their* unstressed vowels in rather complex ways—Russian is a good example; but their way is then always different from ours. Furthermore, probably most languages that distinguish stressed and unstressed syllables use the same vowel phonemes in both positions; and still other languages make no such stress distinctions at all, so that the possibility of using different vowels in these two positions does not even arise. In all such cases our English habits are likely to lead us badly astray. We need to pronounce precisely the vowels we hear in the foreign language, even if this seems "queer" because it conflicts so strongly with our English pronunciation habits.

Stress. Our English stress system is something which we need to watch out for in a number of other ways. In English we make extensive use of stress as part of the structure of words, and we have no less than three degrees of it: primary stress (marked /'/), secondary stress (marked /`/), and weak stress (left unmarked). Examples: *réfugèe, Phárisèe* (primary, weak, secondary) vs. *éffigy, fállacy* (primary, weak, weak); or the noun *óverflòw* (primary, weak, secondary) vs. the verb *òverflów* (secondary, weak, primary); or the compound word *bláckbòard* (primary, secondary) vs. the phrase *bláck bóard* (primary, primary). Other languages, such as German, may also use three degrees of stress in much the same way; or, like Spanish, they may use stress in this way but have only two degrees of it (primary and weak); or, like French, they may not use stress at all as part of the structure of words. Particularly in the case of languages like French we must make sure that we do not carry over into the foreign language the constant ups and downs of stress that seem so natural to us in English.

Where stress is used as part of the structure of words, it is traditionally called "word stress." In English we also have another kind of stress, called "sentence stress," which is used in the structure of sentences and parts of sentences. Consider the following examples, where sentence stress is marked with the symbol /°/:

(Neutral)	(1) Jóe wálked °hóme.
(Where did Joe walk to?)	(2) Jóe wálked °hóme.
(How did Joe get home?)	(3) Jóe °wálked hóme.
(Who walked home?)	(4) °Jóe wálked hóme.

In a neutral rendering of the sentence *Joe walked home,* we usually put sentence stress on the word *home,* as in (1). The same placement is used if we want to put the word *home* at the center of attention, as in (2). But if we want to place *walked* at the center of attention, as in (3), then sentence stress falls on this word; and similarly in (4), where *Joe* is at the center of attention.

The following examples will give some idea of the way in which we combine word stress and sentence stress in any given sentence:

Jóe tálks •fást.
Chárlie's tálking •slówly.
Ábernàthy enúnciàtes pe•cúliarly.
Gíve mè the bláck •bóard. (Not the black shingle.)
Gíve mè the •bláck bóard. (Not the white board.)
Gíve mè the •bláckbòard. (Not the eraser.)
Gíve mè the •óther bláck bóard. (Not this black board.)
Gíve mè the •óther bláckbòard. (Not this blackboard.)

Though perhaps most languages use some sort of "sentence stress," there is no reason to expect that they will use it just as we do. And we certainly cannot expect them to use our combination of sentence stress and word stress, as in the above examples.

Pitch. Whereas the term "stress" refers to the relative prominence given to syllables within a word or sentence, the term "pitch" refers to the relative height of the voice. In English we use pitch only as part of the structure of sentences (and parts of sentences). For example, if we say the word *ready* starting off with a moderately high pitch which then falls to a low pitch and fades out, we react to this as having the meaning "statement": *Ready*. But if it starts off with a moderately high pitch, keeps this level, and then flips still a bit higher at the very end, we react to this as having the meaning "question": *Ready?* And if it starts off with a moderately high pitch, keeps this level but does *not* have the little flip upwards at the end, we take this as an indication that the speaker is going to say some more: *Ready* . . . (*set, go!*) Perhaps because pitch is never consistently represented in writing, most of us are quite unaware of the very extensive use we make of it in English. We therefore need to be all the more attentive to the way pitch is used in the foreign language we are learning, since nearly all languages use it—in one way or another—as part of the structure of sentences and parts of sentences.

Though English uses pitch only as part of the structure of sentences, many other languages also use it as part of the structure of words. Pitch used in this way is customarily called "tone," and languages of this sort are called "tone languages." For example, *bobo* with high pitch on the first syllable and low pitch on the second (somewhat like an English statement: *Bobo.*) may be one word with one meaning; *bobo* with low pitch on the first syllable and high pitch on the second (somewhat like an English question of surprise: *Bobo!?*) may be another word with quite another meaning; and *bobo* with high pitch on both syllables (somewhat like an incomplete English statement: *Bobo . . .*) may be still a third word with still a third meaning. Where each syllable within a word has a particular pitch level, this is customarily called a "register." There may be two such registers in the language: high and low; or three: high, mid, low; or even four: raised high, lowered high, raised low, lowered low (or whatever terms one chooses to use). Such "tone register" languages are common in Africa and among the Indian languages of the Western Hemisphere.

Another way of using pitch as part of word structure is to have rises and falls occur *within* a single syllable, rather than from one syllable to the next; such languages are called "contour tone languages." Here such a syllable as *ma* with a fall from high to low (somewhat like an English statement: *Ma.*) may be one word with one meaning; the same syllable with a rise from low to high (somewhat like an English question of surprise: *Ma!?*) may be another word with quite another meaning; and so on. Such pitch contours are customarily referred to by number: 1st tone, 2nd tone, 3rd tone, etc., up to (apparently) a maximum of seven. Contour tone languages are common in East Asia; the classic example is Chinese.

Because the use of pitch as part of the structure of words is so unfamiliar to speakers of English, the student who needs to learn such a language will do well to consult a special book on the topic: Kenneth L. Pike, *Tone Languages,* Ann Arbor: University of Michigan Press, 1948.

Timing and rhythm. Though the normal speaker is usually at least dimly aware of the ways he uses stress and pitch in English, he is often totally unaware of the timing and rhythm which he constantly employs. Consider the following three sentences:

(1) Jóhn   rúns   •fást.
(2) Jóhnny's   wálking   •slówly.
(3) Jónathan's láboring •háppily.

With only a little exaggeration we can say that it takes the same length of time to pronounce each of these three sentences—despite the fact that (1) contains three syllables, (2) six syllables, and (3) nine syllables. Now consider the following two sentences:

(4) Néwmàrk   bláckbàlls   •Cánfield.
(5) Ábernàthy's   álternàting   •bábysìtters.

Each of these clearly takes more time to say than any of the first three—though (4) has no more syllables than (2) and has fewer than (3). And (4) and (5) both take about the same length of time to say—despite the fact that (5) has twice as many syllables as (4).

What explanation can we give for the "timing" of these sentences? Why should the first three have approximately the same timing, despite the fact that the number of syllables in them varies from three to nine? The feature common to all three of these sentences is the fact that each contains the same number of primary stresses, namely three; and this must be the explanation. However, secondary stress also plays a role in timing: sentences (4) and (5) take more time to say than the first three because they contain, besides three primary stresses, three secondary stresses. (They would take even more time if all six of these stresses were primary; witness such a sentence as *Óld mén nów gét móre •páy.*) All of these examples show clearly that English has what is called "stress-timed rhythm." In terms of time units we can say, very roughly, that each primary stress counts for one unit, each sentence stress for a bit more than one unit, and each secondary stress for a bit less than one unit; whereas weak stress counts hardly at all.

Though some foreign languages have stress-timed rhythm similar to that of English, a great many have instead what is called "syllable-timed rhythm"—where each syllable, whether stressed or unstressed (or simply indifferent to stress), takes up approximately the same amount of time. A good example is Spanish. In pronouncing such a sentence as *¿Cómo se llama usted?* 'What's your name?', we are naturally inclined to give the stress-timed rhythm of English and to say it with three time units corresponding to the three strong stresses: *¿COmo se LLAma usTED?* But Spanish speakers give it syllable-timed rhythm, despite the three strong stresses, and instead say something which we can perhaps indicate by writing: *có-mo-se-llá-maus-téd.* If we can imitate this "pattering" rhythm of Spanish, we will avoid the jerkiness which our stress-timed rhythm wrongly gives it, and our Spanish will sound immensely better. It will sound queer to us, of course; but only if we *do* make it sound queer will there be any possibility that we are actually saying it the Spanish way.

Chapter Five

Sentences

What kinds of sentences may the learner expect to find in the language he is studying? Here it is no longer possible, as it was in the preceding chapter, to run through the sorts of things we say in English and give hints as to how a foreign language may differ. The sentence types of languages differ far too much for this. Nevertheless, we can make a good many comments of a general nature, since there seem to be a number of fundamental principles of sentence construction which are shared by all languages, as well as some further details which are shared by a great many. Perhaps the most important thing we can do is to try to shed some light on the following obvious but nevertheless astounding fact: that, in any language, a speaker can produce—and a hearer can understand—sentences which have never been spoken or heard before; and that, indeed, most of the sentences we say and hear are of just this sort. We shall have to find out how this amazing flexibility is possible.

The first question to ask about sentences is: In the language I am learning, how can I tell when a speaker has come to the end of a sentence? What are the linguistic signals which make this clear? To test this in English, perform the following experiment: Try saying *It's raining* in such a way as to signal to a hearer (1) the fact that you are through, and that he can start talking; and (2) the fact that you are *not* through, and that he should *not* yet start talking. We have, in general, two ways of signaling completion, and one way of signaling incompletion:

(1a) It's raining.   /↓/
(1b) It's raining?   /↑/
(2) It's raining, . . . /|/

At the end of (1a) the voice glides down to a low pitch level and then fades out; if we are then going on with a further sentence, we usually make a slight pause. This "fall and fade" is indicated above by the symbol /↓/. At the end of (1b) the voice stays on a high pitch and then, at the very end, has a little rise or flip upwards. This rise is indicated with the symbol /↑/. This of course signals not only that we are through with our sentence, but also that we are asking a question—the type of question which the hearer can answer with *yes* or *no*. (If we had been asking a question which required a more specific answer, we would have used some such question word as *who, where, when, why;* and then we would most likely have used the same /↓/ as in *It's raining.*) At the end of (2), the voice glides down to nearly as low a pitch as in (1a); but then, instead of fading out, it stays at this low pitch for an instant. Even if we then make a pause, the fact that we did not have any "fade" in our voice is a signal to our hearer that we are not through with our sentence. Indeed, if we do not go on with the rest of it, the effect is much the same as when someone hums a tune but stops on the next to last note: the listener is convinced that there is more to follow. We can call this third type of intonation, signaling incompletion, "sustained" intonation; in the example above it is indicated by means of the symbol /|/.

English, then, typically signals completion (and hence the end of a sentence) either by means of the "fall and fade" intonation /↓/ or, in the case of a question requiring a yes-or-no answer, by means of the "rise" intonation /↑/; and it typically signals incompletion (and hence *not* the end of a sentence) by means of the "sustained" intonation /|/. But this, of course, is only English. In a foreign language you may find some quite different devices used—both to signal what *is* the end of a sentence, and to signal what is *not* the end of a sentence. The most helpful thing you can do is to play some recordings in the foreign language—conversations, stories, or what-not—and spend some time listening particularly for the signals which are used for completion (end of sentence) and incompletion (not end of sentence). There is no way of knowing beforehand just what you will find. But look for such things, listen to them, and then learn to imitate them. Signals that tell a hearer when a speaker has or has not reached the end of a sentence are obviously among the most important signals there are in a language. Native speakers use and respond to them automatically; we, as foreign learners, must learn to do the same thing.

When we start investigating the various types of sentences that occur in a language, there are first of all a number of kinds which we can better leave out for the moment and postpone for later consideration:

1. Elliptical sentences. These are shortened versions of normal sentence types. Example: "When does the movie begin?"—"*At eight o'clock.*" This is clearly a shortened version of: "The movie begins at eight o'clock." Or: "What are we having for supper?"—"*Hash.*" This is a shortened version of: "We are having hash for supper." Greetings are often of this elliptical type, e.g. "Good morning" (presumably a shortened version of some such thing as: "'I wish you a good morning"). Learn these just as they are, without bothering to figure out what their full forms might be. Sometimes elliptical sentences offer serious learning problems: "I hate spinach."—"*So do I.*" This is a very complex way of shortening the full form: "I hate spinach, too." Such things will have to be learned, but at the start it is better to concentrate on the really basic, productive sentence types.

2. Compound sentences. These are combinations of two (or more) basic sentence types: *My brother's going to New York, but I'm staying home.* In such a case we say that the full sentence consists of two INDEPENDENT CLAUSES (i.e. two potential full sentences), connected by some sort of COORDINATING CONJUNCTION (here, the coordinating conjunction *but*). Such compound sentences cause no particular trouble once we understand the basic sentences of which they are composed; but clearly our first task is to learn the basic sentence types.

3. Complex sentences. Here one sentence has been restructured in such a way that it can be embedded inside another sentence. Example: *I saw him when I was in Chicago.* Such sentences are customarily said to consist of a MAIN CLAUSE (or "independent clause") plus a SUBORDINATE CLAUSE (or "dependent clause"), connected by a SUBORDINATING CONJUNCTION. Clearly, three steps are involved in producing such a sentence: first, we have a normal independent sentence *I was in Chicago;* this is then turned into a subordinate clause by means of the subordinating conjunction *when,* giving ... *when I was in Chicago;* and this is then inserted in what we might call the "time slot" of the independent sentence *I saw him* (TIME), giving *I saw him when I was in Chicago.* Such methods of embedding one sentence inside another will occupy us later on (when we discuss "transformations"), and the language you are learning may do the job in ways very different from those of English; but before we learn how thus to "embed" a normal sentence like *I was in Chicago,* we will do better to learn the normal sentence itself.

Let us now consider a normal, basic English sentence, of the simplest type we can find:

Fire burns.

If we take the forms *fire* and *burns* and put them together in the order *burns fire,* the result is quite meaningless. We have added nothing whatever by arranging the two forms in this way; they mean no more together than they did separately; the whole is no greater than the sum of the parts. But if we put them together in the opposite order, the result is very different: *fire burns.* Here each form retains its separate meaning, and we have also added an element of meaning by the very fact of arranging them in this order. This time the whole *is* greater than the sum of the parts. When two forms are combined in this way, they are said to form a CONSTRUCTION; the added element of meaning is called the CONSTRUCTIONAL MEANING. We can diagram this as follows:

Here the little circle represents the construction, and the lines running from it lead to the CONSTITUENTS of the construction. The concept "construction" is *the* fundamental one of grammar; grammar itself is the study of constructions.

If we now compare *Fire burns* with such further sentences as *Water boils, Snow melts, Milk spoils,* we see that these latter are also constructions, and that they are constructions of exactly the same type: NOUN plus VERB, arranged in each case in the same order. If we abbreviate SENTENCE as "S," NOUN as "N," and VERB as "V," we can write the following formula for all sentences of this type:

$$S \rightarrow N + V$$

This can be read as: Rewrite SENTENCE as NOUN plus VERB. Such a formula allows us to think of the grammatical code of English as a kind of sentence-generating machine: we feed in a noun and a verb, and out comes a sentence.

Though this sentence-generating device is disarmingly simple, a little thought will show that it is also extraordinarily powerful and productive. It means that, theoretically, we can put any noun in the slot "N" and any verb in the slot "V" and thereby get a sentence. Given 1000 nouns and 1000 verbs, we can thus produce 1000×1000 or a million sentences. The only limitations are semantic ones: at the moment we can make no use of *Fire boils,* but perhaps some day we shall need to. If so, the sentence will be there, ready and waiting for us, and we shall understand it immediately. Whatever the limitations, we have made a good first step in trying to find out how it is possible for people to say and understand sentences which have never been said before.

We noted above that the constituents of the construction *Fire burns* are the noun *fire* and the verb *burns.* Let us now consider an expanded version of this sentence: *The fire is burning.* What are the constituents of *this* sentence? If we consider only words (and hence do not break *is* down into *i-* +-*s*, and *burning* into *burn* + -*ing*), the ULTIMATE CONSTITUENTS are of course *the, fire, is, burning.* In terms of grammatical structure, however, the IMMEDIATE CONSTITUENTS are *the fire* and *is burning.* That is to say, in the sentence *The fire is burning,* the PHRASES *the fire* and *is burning* play the same grammatical roles as do the WORDS *fire* and *burns* in the sentence *Fire burns.* Letting "NP" stand for NOUN PHRASE and "VP" for VERB PHRASE, we can now give a more inclusive formula which will cover both types of sentences:

$$S \rightarrow NP + VP$$

To this there must be added an indication of the two ways in which we can rewrite "NP" and "VP":

$$\text{NP} \rightarrow \begin{Bmatrix} \text{noun} \\ \text{article} + \text{noun} \end{Bmatrix}$$

$$\text{VP} \rightarrow \begin{Bmatrix} \text{verb} \\ \text{auxiliary} + \text{verb} \end{Bmatrix}$$

The above formulas are valuable in that they show us how a large number of sentences can be generated. But their value goes far beyond this: they not only permit us to generate sentences; they also provide a structural description of each such sentence, in terms of immediate constituents. If, for example, we use these formulas to generate the sentences *Fire burns* and *The fire is burning*, they give us the following phrase-structure diagrams:

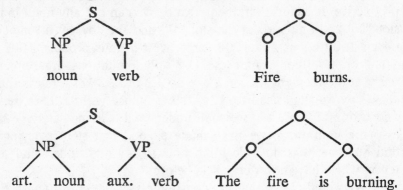

Such diagrams show clearly how each word is related to each other word. Every basic sentence type of English, we can assume, has the immediate constituents "NP" and "VP." The relationship of "NP" to "S" is that of SUBJECT OF THE SENTENCE; and the relationship of "VP" to "S" is that of PREDICATE OF THE SENTENCE.

These formulas are deficient in two respects: they fail to account, first, for the *-ing* of *burn-ing* and, second, for the *-s* of *burn-s* and *i-s*. Though with a little ingenuity we could revise the formulas to take care of all these items, let us consider here only the *-s* of *burn-s*. This is, in effect, a special device to show that the noun of the NP and the verb of the VP are linked together in a construction. It always appears (in English) when the noun of the NP is 3rd person singular and the verb of the VP is in the present tense: *Fire burn-s, Water boil-s*, etc. This type of grammatical linkage is called AGREEMENT (or "concord"), and the verb of the predicate is said to AGREE with the noun of the subject. Many languages which have the "NP + VP" construction show very extensive agreement of this sort. A verb may have six or more different forms depending on the person (1st, 2nd, 3rd) and number (singular, plural—perhaps also dual) of the subject; and it may show this agreement in half a dozen or more tenses, moods, and so on. In still other languages the noun of the subject may belong to a particular class, type, or GENDER (masculine, feminine, neuter; animate, inanimate; or half a dozen or more genders), and the verb of the predicate may then have to contain a morpheme which indicates agreement with this gender.

The concept IMMEDIATE CONSTITUENT mentioned above is extremely helpful in grammatical analysis, and the term itself needs to be used so often that it is customary to abbreviate it to "IC." We need it, for example, to discuss the relationship between *the* and *fire* in the phrase *the fire*. Here we find that one of the IC's (*fire*) belongs to a class of words ("noun") which can perform the same grammatical function (that of "subject of the sentence") as the phrase as a whole, i.e. one can say both *Fire burns* and *The fire burns*. However, the other IC (*the*) belongs to a class of words ("article") which can *not* perform the same grammatical function ("subject of the sentence") as the phrase as a whole, since there is no such sentence as *The burns*. Of the two IC's in the phrase *the fire*, one is therefore central and the other is subordinate to it. In such cases it is customary to say that the central IC (*fire*) is the HEAD of the construction, and that any subordinate IC (*the*) is an ATTRIBUTE which MODIFIES the head. The concept "immediate constituent" also allows us to note the very different relationship between the two IC's of *is burning*. Here neither IC is either head or attribute. There is no basic sentence type such as *The fire is* (this can of course occur in answer to such a question as *What is burning?*, but it is then elliptical for *The fire is burning*); and there is no sentence type at all such as *The fire burning*.

Consider now a sentence such as the following:

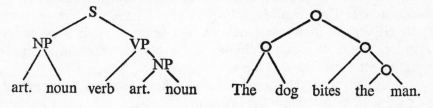

Here we have hit upon an extraordinarily ingenious and economical device. Here we find that a single type of form, an "NP," can appear at two different places and in two different functions. The "NP of S" (*the dog*) is, as before, the SUBJECT OF THE SENTENCE; but the "NP of VP" (*the man*) is the OBJECT OF THE VERB. This means that, instead of requiring us to use a different type of form for every different grammatical function, English allows us to use a single type of form in two (and more) grammatical functions: an "NP" can function both as subject of the sentence and as object of the verb. Now, given 1000 nouns and 1000 verbs, we can (theoretically) form $1000 \times 1000 \times 1000$ or a billion different sentences, since any noun can appear in either of two different grammatical slots.

We pay a price for this, however: we must now add something to the grammar which allows us to tell when an "NP" is functioning in which way. As we saw earlier, English does this largely by means of word order: *The dog bites the man* vs. *The man bites the dog*. Latin uses quite a different device, known as GOVERNMENT. Here a noun must always appear in some particular shape (called a CASE) to show whether it is functioning as "subject of sentence" or as "object of verb." The subject of a Latin sentence is always in the nominative case; and the object of a Latin verb is always in some other case—the accusative, dative, ablative, or genitive, depending on the class of the particular verb. The verb *mordet* 'bites,' for example, governs an object in the accusative. Hence the nominative NP *canis* 'dog,' the accusative NP *virum* 'man,' and the accusative-governing verb *mordet* 'bites' can be combined in any order whatever and give the meaning 'dog bites man': *canis virum mordet, virum canis mordet, canis mordet virum, virum mordet canis, mordet canis virum, mordet virum canis,* etc. Similarly, the accusative NP *canem* 'dog,' the nominative NP *vir* 'man,' and the same verb *mordet* can be combined in any order whatever and give the meaning 'man bites dog': *canem vir mordet, vir canem mordet, canem mordet vir, vir mordet canem, mordet canem vir, mordet vir canem,* etc. The price which English pays for the freedom of using an NP in two different functions is a sharp restriction on word order. The price which Latin pays is the constant necessity of indicating the particular case a noun is in.

A still more striking example of flexibility and economy of grammatical structure is the following:

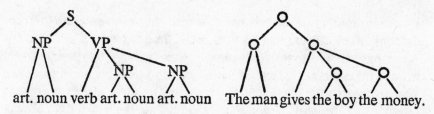

art. noun verb art. noun art. noun   The man gives the boy the money.

Here a single type of filler, "NP," is used for no less than three different functional slots. The "NP of S" (*the man*) is again the subject of the sentence; the *first* "NP of VP" (*the boy*) is the so-called INDIRECT OBJECT of the verb; and the *second* "NP of VP" (*the money*) is the so-called DIRECT OBJECT of the verb. Theoretically, still given only 1000 nouns and 1000 verbs, we can now form no less than $1000 \times 1000 \times 1000 \times 1000$ or a trillion different sentences. The limitations on word order are now of course even stricter than before. Furthermore, limitations of another sort now begin to become very obvious: the slots "subject" and "indirect object" are typically limited to nouns denoting some sort of animate being (*man, boy*, etc.); the slot "direct object" is typically limited to nouns denoting some sort of inanimate object (*money, book*, etc.); and the slot "verb" is typically limited to such meanings as those of *give, send, bring, tell*, etc. Notice that these are the semantic interpretations which we would normally give to the nonsense forms in such a sentence as *The tove gyres the mome the wabe.*

Still a fourth grammatical function of "NP" is illustrated by the following sentence (where "PLACE" stands for "adverbial expression of place," and "prp." is an abbreviation for "preposition"):

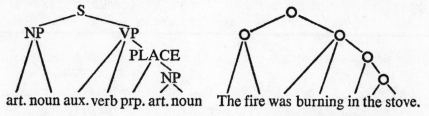

art. noun aux. verb prp. art. noun   The fire was burning in the stove.

In order to mark this particular use of an NP, English grammar uses not word order but the special type of function word called "preposition." An NP which is in construction with a preposition is said to be the OBJECT OF THE PREPOSITION. If the language you are learning has a case system, you may find that some of its prepositions take an object in one case, and some of its prepositions an object in another case; and perhaps also that a given class of prepositions takes objects in two or more different cases, with different meanings. In German, for example, *um* belongs to the class that always takes an accusative object: *um den Ofen* 'around the stove'; *von* belongs to the class that always takes a dative object: *von dem Ofen* 'from the stove'; *innerhalb* belongs to the class that always takes a genitive object: *innerhalb des Ofens* 'inside the stove'; and *in* belongs to the class which takes objects in either accusative or dative, with a difference in meaning: accusative *in den Ofen* 'into the stove,' dative *in dem Ofen* 'in the stove.'

If we look back at the sentences given above as illustrations, we will find that they show another grammatical feature which lends great flexibility to human language. Their elements are arranged in a HIERARCHICAL ORDER: they consist of slots within slots within slots, etc. In *The fire was burning in the stove,* for example, the slots "article" (*the*) and "noun" (*stove*) occur within the slot "NP"; this, in turn, occurs within the slot "place"; this, in turn, occurs within the slot "VP"; and this, finally, occurs within the slot "S," i.e. the entire sentence.

In discussing these sample basic sentence types of English, we have *not* intended to imply that all languages behave in just this way. They most emphatically do not. Our purpose has been rather to mention some general principles of grammatical structure which the learner may expect to find in the language he is studying: constructions; the use of word order as a signal of grammatical structure; some kind of parts of speech system, including a distinction between content words (e.g. nouns, verbs) and function words (e.g. auxiliaries, articles, prepositions); immediate constituents; head and attribute; the use of a given type of form in two or more different functional slots; and the use of slots within slots within slots, etc. (Where a slot within a slot is a whole sentence, this gives the type of "embedded sentence" discussed below on pages 84-86.)

Though you will probably find in the language you are learning something pretty close to our "NP + VP" type of sentence, you may also find other basic types. A common one is the so-called "equational sentence," with the structure "NP + NP." Compare Russian *Iván stud'ént* 'Ivan is a student,' schematically simply "Ivan student." You will certainly find that the word order of the language you are learning is different from that of English. In Japanese the verb is at the end; in some languages it is at the beginning; in German it has to be (in a statement) in second position—though

74

some forms of the verb (infinitive, past participle) must be at the end. Though you will probably find that the language you are learning contains, in one way or another, noun-like words and verb-like words, as well as noun-modifiers and verb-modifiers, you should not necessarily expect to find anything quite like our prepositions, and you can be a bit surprised if you find things like our articles (*the, a/an*)—though you may find them tacked on behind the noun rather than put in front of it. Despite all such differences, however, you will almost certainly find the various grammatical principles mentioned in the preceding paragraph, plus perhaps such other things as agreement, government, genders, and cases.

Once you have tentatively identified a few basic sentence types, in their simplest forms, you can start to build some extremely effective learning devices of the type which have recently come to be called PATTERN DRILLS. Our discussion of grammar thus far (and we shall have more to say later) allows you at this stage to develop the following kinds of pattern drills:

(1) Filling slots. Suppose you have identified some such sentence type as: *The man buys a book.* This has the basic structure "NP + verb + NP," with three slots. See how many things you can put into the first NP slot: (   ) *buys a book.* Now try the verb slot: *The man* (   ) *a book.* What will fit in here? Now try the second NP slot: *The man buys* (   ).

(2) Varying slots. Continue with the same sentence type, but now try such variations as *the men* instead of *the man* (assuming that your language has a distinction between singular and plural). Does the verb show agreement with the noun of the subject slot? Now vary the third slot, using such things as *the book, a book, the books, books, this book, that book,* etc. Finally, try varying the middle slot, *buys;* this will probably yield the richest results of all. Consider all the things which English can put in the slot *The man* (   ) *the book:*

buys/bought	will/would buy
is/was buying	will/would be buying
has/had bought	will/would have bought
has/had been buying	will/would have been buying
does/did buy	

(For any occurrence of *will/would* we can also use *shall/should, can/could, may/might,* or *must.*) You may not find anything as complicated as this; or it may be vastly more complicated. If you find a lot, don't tackle everything at once. Work on one manageable bit at a time.

(3) Adding slots. What can be added to a sentence like *The man bought the book*? Can you add adverbial expressions of time? (*Yesterday, last night, Monday.*) Or adverbial expressions of place? (*Here, there, in a store, in Vladivostok.*) Change it to: *The man reads the book.* Now how about adverbial expressions of manner? (*Quickly, slowly, eagerly, gladly, without his glasses.*) When you add these things, do they occur in any fixed position, e.g. time expressions in one position, place expressions in another, manner expressions in another?

(4) Deleting slots. Take a sentence like: *The fire was burning brightly.* Can any slots be deleted? This drill is of course the opposite of number (3) above, and it cannot be applied to sentences with a minimum number of slots. But the only way to find out whether a sentence is minimal is to try out such deletions on the foreign speaker with whom you are working.

(5) Expanding slots. From the sentences you have already worked on, can you pick up any examples of things like "The fire was burning *very* brightly"? This would mean expanding the slot *brightly* to *very brightly.* This is of course "adding a slot," as in (3) above, though since it is at a lower level it is sometimes helpful to think of it as an expansion of an already existing slot rather than as the addition of a new one.

(6) Contracting slots. This is the reverse of (5). It is worth applying so that you can understand the IC's of slots within slots within slots, etc. For example, from the sentence *My brother reads much more quickly,* one first deletes the *much* and then the *more,* and cannot delete them in the reverse order. This is of course "deleting a slot," as in (4) above, though at a lower IC level.

Thus far we have been discussing only sentences of the most basic types. If they went beyond the category "basic" it was only because they contained more than a bare minimum of slots. Before discussing some more complex types, we first need to introduce three further grammatical concepts. Consider the following pair of sentences:

(1) The policeman shot the man.
(2) The man was shot by the policeman.

Though we intuitively feel that these are somehow two versions of the "same thing," if we should make structural diagrams of them they would look very different. In (1) the subject is *the policeman,* whereas in (2) the subject is *the man*—even though we still know that the policeman was the one who did the shooting. In (1) the verb has an object *the man,* whereas in (2) it does not—even though we still know that the man was the one who got shot. Even the verbs disagree: *shot* vs. *was shot.* If structural diagrams fail to show the similarity in meaning which we all feel exists between these two sentences, this can only be because something is badly missing in our structural diagrams. And indeed something *is* missing —though it must be shown in quite a different way.

The problem which faces us in this pair of sentences is a very general one; we could find it over and over again in countless other pairs of sentences. It is this: *as we understand* these two sentences, they are almost the same; but *as we say* these two sentences, they are quite different. We can solve this problem by assuming, for any sentence, two levels of grammatical structure: a DEEP STRUCTURE, which represents the way we understand the sentence; and a SURFACE STRUCTURE, which represents the way we say the sentence. Grammatical elements are arranged quite differently in these two kinds of structure. In the deep structure they are arranged in HIERARCHICAL ORDER, corresponding to the structural description of each sentence, in terms of immediate constituents. This type of arrangement corresponds to the way we *understand* the sentence. In the surface structure grammatical elements are arranged in LINEAR ORDER. This type of arrangement corresponds to the way we *say* the sentence, with one element following the other, through the dimension of time (as we speak). In between the deep structure and the surface structure we can assume a set of TRANSFORMATIONAL RULES which convert the hierarchical order of elements in the deep structure into the linear order of elements in the surface structure, and vice versa.

Now we can return to our two sentences. Sentence (1), *The policeman shot the man,* is customarily called "active"; sentence (2), *The man was shot by the policeman,* is customarily called "passive." Because we understand these two sentences as having the same basic meaning, we can assume that they also have the same basic deep structure—with the same grammatical elements in the same hierarchical arrangement. They differ only in the fact that sentence (2) contains an element "passive" which is lacking in sentence (1). *Without* this element "passive," transformational rules give the linear surface structure that lies behind the spoken sentence (1) *The policeman shot the man. With* this element "passive," transformational rules give the very different linear surface structure that lies behind the spoken sentence (2) *The man was shot by the policeman.* In sentence (1), *the policeman* is the subject both in the deep structure and in the surface structure; and *the man* is the object of the verb both in the deep structure and in the surface structure. In sentence (2), the deep structure subject is still *the policeman* (this is the way we understand the sentence), but in the surface structure transformational rules have converted this into the so-called "agent expression" *by the policeman;* and the deep structure object of the verb is still *the man* (this is again the way we understand the sentence), though in the surface structure transformational rules have converted this into the subject.

The transformational principle—deep structure vs. surface structure, connected by transformational rules—plays an essential role in the grammars of all languages. The following paragraphs indicate some of the transformations that we find in simple English sentences.

(1) Statement vs. General question. *Without* the element "question," transformational rules convert the deep structure *John + live here* into the surface structure *John lives here. With* the element "question," they convert the deep structure *John + live here + Question* into the surface structure *Does John live here?* Note the addition of the meaningless "dummy" auxiliary verb *do.* If the deep structure already contains an auxiliary verb, however, the dummy *do* is not added. Hence the deep structure *John + can live here + Question* gives the surface structure *Can John live here?* Here it is the surface word order alone, without the dummy *do,* which signals the fact that this is a question. The dummy *do* is also not added if the deep structure verb is *be:* deep structure *John + be here + Question,* surface structure *Is John here?* The dummy *do* is optional if the verb of the deep structure is *have.* Deep structure *you + have a pencil + Question* may be transformed in the surface structure either into *Do you have a pencil?* or into *Have you a pencil?* (Where *have* functions as an auxiliary verb, however, *do* is never used: deep structure *you + see John + Perfect + Question* is always transformed into surface structure *Have you seen John?*, never into *Do you have seen John?*)

(2) Statement vs. Specific question. In a general question, there is no particular grammatical slot that is being questioned; instead, the sentence as a whole is being questioned. In a specific question, on the other hand, the notion "question" is directed at some specific grammatical slot; and for this purpose a specific QUESTION WORD is used. Consider the following examples. In a statement the grammatical slot "place" may be filled, for example, by the word *here:* deep structure *John + live here,* surface structure *John lives here.* In a general question the deep structure is the same except for the addition of the element "question": *John + live here + Question,* surface structure *Does John live here?* In a specific question, on the other hand, it is precisely the slot "place" that is being questioned: deep structure *John + live Place? + Question;* surface structure *Where does John live?*

English has specific question words for the following grammatical slots:

Nominal:	personal	who/whom
	impersonal	what (e.g. *What is this?*)
	possessive	whose (e.g. *Whose is this?*)
	demonstrative	which (e.g. *Which is this?*)
Adjectival:	demonstrative	which, what (e.g. *which hat, what hat?*)
	possessive	whose (e.g. *whose hat?*)
	descriptive	what kind of
Adverbial:	time	when
	place	where
	manner	how
	cause	why

(3) Statement vs. Command. *Without* the element "command," transformational rules convert the deep structure *you + close the door* into the surface structure *You close the door. With* the element "command," they convert the deep structure *you + close the door + Command* into the surface structure *Close the door,* i.e. they delete the 2nd person pronoun *you.* (Our deep structure descriptions of statements and questions have thus far been incomplete in that they have omitted the element "tense." It is more accurate to say that the deep structure underlying *You close the door* is *you +*

close the door + *Present;* contrast *You closed the door,* where the underlying deep structure is *you* + *close the door* + *Past.* The presence of "tense" in statements and questions, plus the fact that commands are "tenseless," is nicely illustrated by the English verb *be.* The deep structure *you* + *be here at six* + *Present* gives *You are here at six;* the deep structure *you* + *be here at six* + *Past* gives *You were here at six;* and the deep structure *you* + *be here at six* + *Command* gives *Be here at six.*) Note that ordinary commands are limited to sentences in which the deep structure subject is *you.* English also has another sort of "command" in which the deep structure subject is *we:* deep structure *we* + *go* + *Command,* surface structure *Let us go.*

(4) Plain vs. Emphatic. *Without* the element "emphatic," transformational rules convert the deep structure *John* + *live here* into the surface structure *John lives here. With* the element "emphatic," they convert the deep structure *John* + *live here* + *Emphatic* into the surface structure *John does live here.* The presence or absence of the dummy auxiliary verb *do* is governed by the same rules as in (2) above.

(5) Positive vs. Negative. *Without* the element "negative," transformational rules convert the deep structure *John* + *live here* into the surface structure *John lives here. With* the element "negative," they convert the deep structure *John* + *live here* + *Negative* into the surface structure *John does not live here.* The presence or absence of the dummy auxiliary verb *do* is again governed by the same rules as in (2) above.

(6) Active vs. Passive. This is the type of transformation we have already discussed. *Without* the element "passive," transformational rules convert the deep structure *the policeman* + *shoot the man* into the surface structure *The policeman shot the man. With* the element "passive," they convert the deep structure *the policeman* + *shoot the man* + *Passive* into the surface structure *The man was shot by the policeman.* Note that "passive" can occur only in sentences in which the verb has a direct object. It cannot occur in such deep structures as *John* + *live here,* or *the trip* + *last three days.*

(7) Full form vs. Substitute form. Consider the following example. In answer to the question: "What were John and Mary doing in the jewelry store?", we can reply either: (a) *"John was* buying *Mary* a wedding ring," or (b) *"He* was buying *her* a wedding ring." Here *he* and *her* serve as SUBSTITUTES for the full words *John* and *Mary*, respectively. Since we *understand* sentence (b) as having the same meaning as sentence (a), we can assume that both have essentially the same deep structure. The only difference is that, in sentence (b), we have chosen to use substitute forms rather than full forms. Once we have done this, transformational rules convert *John* into the surface structure word *he*, and *Mary* into the surface structure word *her*. Substitute words, in contrast to full words, have minimal semantic content. A reasonably complete list of English substitute words, arranged according to the types of slots they fill, includes the following:

Nominal:	personal	he, she ⎱ they
	impersonal	it ⎰
	possessive	mine, yours, his, hers, etc.
	demonstrative	this, that (e.g. *This is* . . .)
	modified	one (*this one, the big one*, etc.)
Adjectival:	demonstrative	this, that (e.g. *this man*)
	possessive	my, your, his, her, etc.
	descriptive	such
Adverbial:	time	now, then
	place	here, there
	manner	thus, so
	cause	hence, therefore

Notice how closely these substitute words parallel the question words listed in (2) above. English also has a word *do*, which substitutes for the entire predicate of a sentence. An example is: "Do you *swear to tell the truth, the whole truth, and nothing but the truth, so help you God?"* In the answer "I *do*," the word *do* serves as a substitute for the entire predicate *swear to tell the truth, the whole truth, and nothing but the truth, so help me God.* Two further substitute words are *yes* and *no. Yes* serves as a substitute for an entire sentence; *no* serves as a substitute for an entire sentence + "negative."

(8) Deletion by transformation. Consider the passive sentence *The man was shot.* As we understand this sentence, the deep structure has a kind of "dummy subject." That is to say, no information is given as to just who did the shooting; yet we know that *someone* must have done it. We can symbolize this by writing the deep structure as follows: (*someone*) + *shoot the man* + *Passive,* using the parenthesized notation (*someone*) to indicate the dummy subject. Transformational rules now convert this to the surface structure *The man was shot,* with no indication of who did the shooting; that is to say, the dummy subject (*someone*) has been completely deleted from the surface structure. (Note the difference between this sentence and the sentence *The man was shot by someone.* Here the deep structure subject is the indefinite prououn *someone;* but it is not a "dummy subject," and it is therefore not deleted from the surface structure.)

(9) Stylistic transformations. We have already pointed out that surface structure word order can serve as a signal of grammatical deep structure. In *The dog bit the man* vs. *The man bit the dog,* it is word order alone which tells us which NP (*the dog, the man*) is functioning as the subject of the sentence, and which is functioning as the object of the verb. It is also word order alone which distinguishes the statement *John can live here* from the question *Can John live here?* There are many other cases, however, where word order signals not grammatical meaning but merely shades of stylistic meaning. Example: "*Last Tuesday* I saw Mary in New York" vs. "I saw Mary *last Tuesday* in New York" vs. "I saw Mary in New York *last Tuesday.*" Here transformational rules permit us to place the time expression *last Tuesday* in any one of three different surface positions, with no essential change in meaning.

In the preceding discussion we have considered only the grammatical structure of English. Though all of the distinctions mentioned will probably also occur in the language you are learning, they may be made in quite different ways. (1) If you are lucky, the difference between a Statement and a General Question will be signalled only by intonation, as things would be in English if the normal Question corresponding to the Statement *He lives here* were simply *He lives here?* Or your language may make use of word order, as in French *Vous comprenez* 'You understand' vs. *Comprenez-vous?* 'Do you understand?' Or it may simply add a little question particle, as in Japanese *Wakarimasu ka?* '(Do you) understand?' vs. *Wakarimasu* '(I, you) understand.' (2) The difference between a Statement and a Specific Question will almost certainly be signaled by the use of a set of special Question Words. This seems to be true of all languages, and such Question Words are therefore the kinds of things you should try to learn almost from the very start. (3) As for the difference between a Statement and a Command, this may very well be signaled by the use of a special set of "imperative" verb forms. (4) The difference between Plain and Emphatic will probably not be signaled by the use of a dummy verb like English *do;* more likely there will be a special word for this, as in German *Er wohnt hier* 'He lives here' vs. emphatic *Er wohnt doch hier* 'He does too live here.' (5) The notion "negative" may be expressed by a special word like English *not,* as in German "Ich verstehe Sie *nicht*" 'I do *not* understand you'; or it may be expressed by a pair of words, as in French "Je *ne* vous comprend *pas*"; or it may be expressed by a simple little element like the *-eñ* of Japanese "Wakarimase*ñ*" '(I, you) do not understand.' (6) You will probably find a distinction between Active and Passive, though it may be expressed in a way quite different from that of English. Cf. Latin *occīdit* 'he kills' vs. *occīditur* 'he is killed.' (7) The Substitute Words, particularly the Personal Pronouns, may be very different from those of English. German distinguishes between Plain Singular *du* 'you,' Plain Plural *ihr* 'you,' and Polite Singular/Plural *Sie* 'you.' French distinguishes between Plain Singular *tu* and Plain Plural, Polite Singular/Plural *vous.* Japanese applies the Plain vs. Polite distinction to the 1st person as well: Plain *boku* 'I' vs. Polite *watakusi* 'I.' (The terms Plain and Polite refer here to the speaker's attitude toward his hearer, not toward himself.) Many languages distinguish between an "Inclusive 1st Person Plural" (I and others, including my hearers) and an "Exclusive 1st Person Plural" (I and others, excluding my hearers).

The grammatical structures that we have been considering thus far allow us to account for many millions, even billions, of English sentences. Yet there is one aspect of grammar that we have not yet considered: the fact that, in English and every other language, it is theoretically possible to say an unlimited number of sentences. For example, any sentence we can imagine can always have something further added to it; hence the number of possible sentences is unlimited.

How are we to account for this extraordinary property of human language? One type of device which accounts for an unlimited number of anything is known, in mathematics, as a RECURSIVE DEVICE. Such a device permits a system to feed upon itself over and over again, theoretically without limit. We can compare this with a mirror, which reflects a man holding a mirror, which reflects a man holding a mirror—and so on and on, without end.

In human language, recursion takes two quite different forms. In COORDINATION, two deep structure sentences (minus those features which make them "complete sentences") are combined so as to produce a single (complete) sentence. In SUBORDINATION, one sentence (minus those features which make it a "complete sentence") is embedded inside another sentence so as to produce a single (complete) sentence. In each case the process is recursive—that is, it can be performed over and over again, theoretically without end.

Coordination. Suppose we start out with the following sentence:

John Ball shot them all.

Then we decide to add some more. We change this into an "almost-sentence" (a sentence minus those features which mark it as "complete"), add on in front of it another almost-sentence *John Scott made the shot,* connect the two with the coordinating conjunction *but,* and then say:

John Scott made the shot,
But John Ball shot them all.

To this we now add the almost-sentence *John Brammer made the rammer,* along with the coordinating conjunction *and.* This gives:

John Brammer made the rammer,
And John Scott made the shot,
But John Ball shot them all.

Coordination can obviously go on and on, as long as we want it to. In the typical case transformational rules will delete parts of successive "almost-sentences" so as to give a more economical "complete sentence." For example, the almost-sentences *he smokes cigars* and *he smokes cigarettes* can be combined by means of *and* so as to give the complete sentence *He smokes cigars and he smokes cigarettes.* It is more likely, however, that we will let transformational rules delete the second occurrence of *he smokes* so as to give *He smokes cigars and cigarettes.*

Subordination. When we transform the structures underlying *He smokes cigars* + *He smokes cigarettes* into *He smokes cigars and cigarettes,* it is easy to see that two (potential) sentences have been combined into one; but we have no way of determining which has been inserted into which. We now need to consider cases in which this question is easily answered—that is, cases in which one almost-sentence has been EMBEDDED into a full-sentence and is SUBORDI-NATE to it. Probably the most famous example of embedding in all of English is the following:

This is the cat	(1) This is the cat.
that killed the rat	(2) The cat killed the rat.
that ate the malt	(3) The rat ate the malt.
that lay in the house	(4) The malt lay in the house.
that Jack built.	(5) Jack built the house.

To the left we give the full sentence, which consists of a series of four successive embeddings. To the right we give the structures which each of the constituent sentences would have if it were used independently as a complete sentence. Sentence (5) is first embedded in sentence (4); the resulting sentence is then embedded in sentence (3); the resulting sentence is then embedded in sentence (2); and the resulting sentence is then embedded in sentence (1). At level (1) *This is the cat* is the MATRIX SENTENCE into which all the rest is embedded; at level (2) *the cat killed the rat* is the matrix sentence into which all the rest is embedded; and so on.

   In describing subordination we need to consider not only (a) the matrix sentence and (b) the embedded sentence, but also (c) the kind of grammatical slot which the embedded sentence fills within the matrix sentence: a nominal slot, an adjectival slot, an adverbial slot, etc. The following are a few examples. (=> 'is transformed into')

(1) The embedded sentence fills a nominal slot.

It is true +	=> It is true *that he will come.*
He will come	Or: *That he will come* is true.
It is uncertain +	=> It is uncertain *whether he will come.*
Will he come?	Or: *Whether he will come* is uncertain.
It is uncertain +	=> It is uncertain *when he will come.*
When will he come?	Or: *When he will come* is uncertain.

(2) The embedded sentence fills an adjectival slot.

We saw the man +	=> We saw the man
The man spoke	*that/who spoke.*
We saw the house +	=> We saw the house
The house burned	*that/which burned.*

(3) The embedded sentence fills an adverbial slot.

I came (*time*) +   => I came *when he came* (or *did*).
    He came (*time*)

I live (*place*) +   => I live *where he lives* (or *does*).
    He lives (*place*)

I work (*manner*) +   => I work *as he works* (or *does*).
    He works (*manner*)

I left (*cause*) +   => I left *because he left* (or *did*).
    He left

In the above examples the embedded sentence still keeps its essential structure, and its subject and verb still have more or less their normal shapes. There are other types of transformations in English, however, where these shapes are changed. One example: *She sees him + He does it => She sees him do it.* Here the *he* of the embedded sentence has been collapsed with the *him* of the matrix sentence, and *does* has been transformed to *do.* Another example: *It surprised us + He resigned the post => His resigning the post surprised us.* Here the embedded sentence has been transformed into an NP which functions as the subject of the matrix sentence. In still other types it is not a whole sentence which is embedded but only the predicate: *It costs a lot + (Someone) lives in the suburbs => Living in the suburbs costs a lot,* or *To live in the suburbs costs a lot,* or *It costs a lot to live in the suburbs.* Here the predicate of the embedded sentence has been transformed into an NP which functions as the subject of the matrix sentence. In the first example it has the shape *living in the suburbs;* in the second, *to live in the suburbs;* in the third, by a further transformation, it is placed at the end and the normal subject slot is filled by the dummy subject *it.*

If we were to continue with further examples of transformations, we would simply be going more and more deeply into English grammar, and this is of course not our purpose. The examples already given are enough to alert you to the kinds of things you may expect to find in the language you are learning. They also make it clear (if further clarification should be needed) how it is possible for us, in any language, to say and understand sentences which have never been said before. All of these transformational rules are part of the "built-in grammatical" code which we carry around inside our heads, and we can call on them at any time to produce or to understand a brand new sentence.

Chapter Six

Words

What is a "word"? Most of us have a pretty strong intuitive feeling that the phonemic sequence /róziz/ consists of one word in "Look at the *roses* here," but that it consists of two words in "I see that *Rose is* here." Indeed, we would probably make our phonemic transcription agree with standard spelling by writing the former as /róziz/ but the latter as /róz iz/, with a space. This is odd, since both examples can be said, and usually are said, in just the same way. What lies behind this strong intuitive feeling that *roses* is one word but that *Rose is* is two words? The answer seems to lie in the very different types of grammatical freedom which the two forms possess. The /iz/ of *Rose is here* can occur not only after nouns like *Rose,* but also after words of almost any part of speech —or, indeed, after nothing at all, as in *Is Rose here?* It is therefore what we call a FREE FORM. The /iz/ of *the roses here,* on the other hand, can occur in just one position: after a noun, as its plural ending. It is therefore what we call a BOUND FORM. This now brings us to the following definitions which satisfy our intuitive feelings quite well. (1) If a free form is composed of free IC's, it is a PHRASE. Examples: *Rose is here* (with the free IC's *Rose* and *is here*); *is here* (with the free IC's *is* and *here*). But (2) if a free form is *not* composed of free IC's, it is a WORD. In *roses,* one of the IC's (*rose*) is, to be sure, free; but the other IC (/-iz/) is bound, and this makes the whole form *roses* a word rather than a phrase.

In any language we study, we will find that its words fall into some sort of PARTS OF SPEECH system: classes of words which are specialized in filling particular types of grammatical slots. The English parts of speech system includes the following classes:

(1) Nouns. These functions as subjects of sentences: "The *man* came," as objects of verbs: "I saw the *man*," as objects of prepositions: "with the *man*," and as heads which can be modified by adjectives and adjective-like attributes: *tall men, the tall man, all these* six *tall men,* etc. Nouns have, in general, four inflected forms: *man, man's, men, men's,* though most of them actually have only two different phonemic shapes: *boy* (= /bói/), *boy's, boys, boys'* (all = /bóiz/).

(2) Verbs. These function as the one indispensable slot in the predicate: "The man *came,*" "I *see* the man." Full verbs (we shall consider auxiliary verbs later) have five inflected forms: *see, sees, saw, seen, seeing,* though most of them actually have only four different phonemic shapes: *look, looks, looked* = *looked, looking.*

(3) Adjectives. These fill the slots "the NOUN is ( )," and "the ( ) NOUN," for example "the man is *tall,*" "the *tall* man." (Some adjective-like words fill only the former slot: "the baby is *asleep,*" but never "the *asleep* baby"; others fill only the latter slot: "the *other* man," but never "the man is *other.*") Some adjectives, though by no means all, are inflected for comparison: *tall, tall-er, tall-est.*

(4) Adverbs in -ly. These fill various adverbial slots, such as "he walked *slowly, quickly, energetically,*" or "he was *barely, fully, completely* conscious."

Three aspects of these classes need to be emphasized. First, the classification itself is quite clear. Even when a word belongs to more than one class (*the table, to table; to clean, very clean*), we know what type to assign it to in any given instance. Second, these are OPEN classes in the sense that they are huge in number and that new ones are being created all the time. (Cf. *sputnik, spacesuit, astronaut*—not yet listed in a very good 1947 dictionary.) Third, these are the four classes which provide the CONTENT WORDS of English: words which are strong in lexical meaning. (They also have grammatical meaning, of course—precisely the meaning which we sum up in the terms "noun," "verb," "adjective," and "adverb.") We may recall that, in *Jabberwocky,* it was these four classes—and only these classes—for which Lewis Carroll was able to substitute nonsense words and still keep the poem grammatically meaningful.

In sharp contrast to these first four parts of speech are the remaining word classes of English. First, the classification itself is not always clear. The word *there* in *There is still time* seems to belong to a class all by itself; so also do such words as *not* and *very*. Even where we can establish relatively clear classes, there is a great deal of overlap: *down* seems to be an adverb in *he fell down* but a preposition in *he fell down the stairs*. Second, whatever classes we can find are CLOSED classes (who can make up a new pronoun or preposition?) and they are all relatively small in number—some consisting of only a handful of items. Third, it is these classes which provide the FUNCTION words of English: words which signal grammatical structure but often do little more than that. (What is the "meaning" of *on* in "I insist *on* that"?) Because they *do* signal the general outlines of grammatical structure, Lewis Carroll could *not* replace them with nonsense forms when he wrote *Jabberwocky*.

The following is one possible classification of these words in English:

(5) Pronouns. These surely include *I/me, we/us, you, he/him, she/her, it, they/them;* but after that it is hard to know just where to stop.

(6) Auxiliary verbs. This class includes *be, have, do* in some uses, e.g. "he *is* working, he *has* worked, he *does* work," but not in "he is *being* funny, we are *having* trouble, he is *doing* it." There are four basic phonemic shapes for *have: have, has, had ＝ had, having;* there are five for *do: do, does, did, done, doing;* and there are no less than eight for *be: be, am, is, are, was, were, been, being*. This class also includes *shall/should, will/would, can/could, may/might, must;* but these are grammatically defective since one cannot say things like *to shall* or *I have shoulded*. The class also includes *need* and *dare* in some uses: auxiliary verb in *he need not do it, he dare not do it*, but full verb in *he does not need to do it, he does not dare to do it*. And the class presumably includes the curious word *ought*, since there is nowhere else to put it.

(7) Articles, determiners, etc. This class includes such words as *the, a/an; this/these, that/those* (or are these also pronouns of some

sort?); *my, your, her,* etc. (but what are *mine, yours, hers*—pronouns?); things like *each, every, no, some, any, much, many, such* (also part pronouns); *other, same;* and a number of further items including, as a special subclass, *one, two, three,* etc. These words are all "adjectival" in the sense that they can modify nouns; on the other hand, one cannot say "the man is *the,* the man is *each,* the man is *other*," as one can with genuine adjectives ("the man is *tall,* the *tall* man").

(8) Prepositions. These include *on, in, off, to, of, from, with,* and a few handfuls of others. What do we do with *off of, instead of, on account of, because of, in front of, in back of, on top of,* etc.? Words? Phrases?

(9) Coordinating conjunctions. Examples have been given in Chapter 5 in the discussion of coordinate transformation: *and, or, but, not only . . . but also, either . . . or, neither . . . nor, both . . . and.*

(10) Subordinating conjunctions. Examples: *if, although, after* (also a preposition), *when* (also a question word), *as* (also a coordinating conjunction), *that* (also a determiner and maybe a pronoun), etc. The class also includes curious things like *once* (*Once we have done this, . . .*).

(11) "Adverbs." This is really a grab bag for whatever is left over. It traditionally includes such diverse items as *here, there; now, then; yesterday, today, tomorrow; so, thus; ever, never; also, too; yes, no; not; almost; very; only.* Words like *ah, oh, damn* are generally classified as "interjections"; but lots of words can be used as interjections. Or is "interjection" a useful class to contain words used *only* as interjections? Perhaps it is a matter of taste. And what of words like *indeed, nevertheless, however, therefore*? Are they "sentence adverbs"? Or a special class of conjunctions?

(12) Question words, and *(13) Substitutes.* These two classes have already been discussed in the preceding chapter. We arrive at them not by observing the grammatical slots that they fill but rather by examining the transformations in which they occur. The class of English question words seems quite clear: *who/whom/whose, what, which, when, where, why, how.* The class of substitutes is clear insofar as it includes personal and impersonal pronouns, but after that it is hard to know just where to stop. We listed *this/these, that/those, one, do, such, now, then, here, there, thus, so, hence,*

therefore. Perhaps we should delete some of these, and probably we should add some others.

What sort of parts of speech system will you find in the language you are learning? How typical is English? In one respect it is not typical at all. Unless you are learning a language *related* to English (one of the Indo-European group), it is highly unlikely that you will find as many parts of speech as we have in English, however one figures them. Though there will probably be noun-like words and verb-like words, there need not be a sharp division into the two parts of speech "noun" and "verb." We find this hard to imagine; and yet we ourselves can "paint" (verb) a house with "paint" (noun). So why have one class of words specialized in the one function, and another specialized in the other function? Why not just one class which can function in both ways? Whereas we take it almost as a matter of divine necessity that a language must have adjectives, it may be that what we think of as adjectives turn out to be verbs in the language you are learning. Instead of saying "The tree is green" why not say something like "The tree greens"? And instead of "the green tree," why not "the greening tree"? We take it for granted that we must say "He ran quickly," using an adverb. But why not "He ran with quickness"?

In three other respects, English *is* more or less typical. First, you can expect to find a set of substitute words in the language you are learning (though not necessarily just like those of English), and you will want to learn these almost from the start. Second, you can expect to find a set of question words; these are also highly useful in early stages of language learning. Third, you may expect to find much the same general arrangement as in English: one, two, or three "open classes" of content words, with (practically speaking) unlimited membership; and then a rather ill-defined assortment of function words, which may or may not fall into distinct classes. The learning problems involved in these two general categories of words are quite different. No one can ever hope to learn all the content words in a language; we simply do the best we can. On the other hand, we *must* learn nearly all the function words, since these are the blood and bone of the language's grammatical structure. You need to be able to handle the foreign language the way we can all handle *Jabberwocky:* understand the function words so that you can at least get the grammatical structure, even if you do not know how all the content slots are filled. A knowledge of the function slots will at least give *some* meaning (the grammatical meaning), and we can hope to fill in the rest later on. On the other hand, even a perfect knowledge of the content slots is of no use if we do not understand how they are put together.

In the language you are studying you can expect not only that words will fall into a number of different classes but also that you may find words with several different types of internal structure. Some will consist simply of a ROOT, i.e. a single morpheme. English examples: *come, friend, but, of.* Others may consist of a STEM plus one or more bound forms or AFFIXES: *friend-s, friend-ly, friend-li-ness, un-friend-li-ness.* This stem may also be a root (a single morpheme), such as the stem of *friend-s, friend-ly;* or it may not be a root because it already contains an affix, e.g. the stem *friendly* in *friendli-ness.* Still other words may consist of two roots (or two stems) marked somehow to show that they are not simply a sequence of words. For example, the English form *bláckbòard* is composed of the two roots *black* and *board,* and the stress pattern "primary + secondary" marks this combination as a single word as against the two-word sequence *bláck bóard.*

When affixes are added to stems, the resulting words may function grammatically in two quite different ways. For example, the words *friend-s* and *friend-ly* both consist of stem plus affix: *friend* + *-s, friend* + *-ly;* and yet we feel intuitively that these are quite different types of constructions. What lies behind this intuitive feeling? There are a number of reasons for it. One is the fact that, when we add *-s* to *friend,* it remains a noun; whereas when we add *-ly* to *friend* the resulting word is not a noun but an adjective. We therefore feel that we have somehow "made a new word." Another reason is the fact that the *-s* of *friends* represents the noun plural morpheme, and in one way or another we can add this to *every* noun (excluding only such oddities as *sheep, deer,* etc.); whereas there are vast numbers of nouns—such as *table, house, tree*—to which we cannot add the affix *-ly.* A still more powerful reason is the fact that the noun plural morpheme is COMPULSORY, whereas the adjectivizing morpheme *-ly* is OPTIONAL. There are countless grammatical situations in which a noun (again excluding the oddities *sheep, deer,* etc.) must show the plural morpheme in one shape or another: *Where are your* (　　)?, *two of the* (　　), etc. On the other hand, there are no situations whatever in which the grammar of English compels us to use an adjective in *-ly:* instead of *a friendly person* one can say *a nice person, a kind person,* etc.

When a word contains a compulsory affix (such as the *-s* of *friends*), it is said to be INFLECTED; when it contains an optional affix (such as the *-ly* of *friendly*), it is said to be DERIVED. Languages vary greatly in the amount of inflection and derivation they show. English has a modest amount of inflection, principally in its nouns: *boy, boy's, boys, boys',* in its verbs: *look, looks, looked, looked, looking,* and in some adjectives: *tall, taller, tallest;* though also in such bits and pieces as *this/these, that/those, I/me/my/mine, she/her/her/hers,* etc. Some languages have a distressing amount of inflection (a few readers may remember the verbs of Greek), others have none at all. On the other hand, all languages seem to have at least some derivation, and many languages—English, for example—have great masses of it.

The learning problems presented by inflection and derivation are quite different. Precisely because they *are* compulsory, inflected forms simply must be learned—though one does not have to learn them all at once. Learning derived forms, on the other hand, can be a much more leisurely business. We can learn the adjective *friendly* even if we do not know the underlying noun stem *friend.* Such a procedure is in part necessary because derivation is in general quite unsystematic; witness such words as *ungainly* and *raffish,* where the affixes *un-, -ly,* and *-ish* are familiar enough, but where the learner would look in vain for the independent underlying stems *gain* and *raff.* In the long run, of course, the learner will want to know how to handle derived forms just as a native speaker does. Especially in the cases of affixes that are highly productive, learning to understand derivation can greatly increase one's practical control of a language. But, as we say, the learning of derivation can be postponed almost indefinitely. The learning of inflection cannot.

Depending on where they are added in relation to a stem, affixes fall into four subtypes:

(1) Prefixes. These are added before the stem. English examples: *de-ceive, per-ceive, con-ceive, un-tie, en-twine, im-polite, re-cóver* 'get well,' *ré-cóver* 'cover again' (all derivational).

(2) Suffixes. These are added after the stem. English examples: *form-s, form-ed, form-ing* (all inflectional), *form-al, formal-ize, formaliz-er* (all derivational). Whereas English derivational affixes may be either prefixes or suffixes, it just so happens that all inflec-

tional affixes are suffixes (and we therefore often speak of them as "endings"). This is not, however, in any sense a necessary arrangement; some languages have inflectional prefixes.

(3) Infixes. These are added inside the stem. Infixation is a very live process in many languages, for example in the Philippine language Ilocano:

		Stem		*Infix*
panaw	'go'	balay	'house'	
		Present		
pumanaw	'he goes'	bumalay	'he builds a house'	-um-
		Past		
pimmanaw	'he went'	bimmalay	'he built a house'	-imm-

Those who remember their Latin will recall that this language shows a few traces of infixation. Compare stem *jug-* in *jugum* 'yoke' and, with infix *-n-*, in *jungō* 'I join'; stem *frag-* in *fragilis* 'breakable' and, with infix *-n-*, in *frangō* 'I break'; stem *tag-* in past participle *tactus* 'touched' (with change of *g* to *c*) and, with infix *-n-*, in *tangō* 'I touch.' In the case of infixation it is of course important to note just where within a stem the infix is inserted. Ilocano *-um-*, *-imm-* are inserted *before* the first vowel of the stem: *p-um-anaw, p-imm-anaw;* Latin *-n-* is inserted *after* the vowel of the stem: *ju-n-gō, fra-n-gō, ta-n-gō.* A rather special case is provided by the Semitic languages. In Arabic, for example, there are large numbers of triconsonantal stems into which an infix may be inserted on both sides of the middle consonant: from the stem *k-t-b* 'write' are formed *katab* 'he wrote' (infix *-a-a-*), *kātib* 'writer' (infix *-ā-i-*), *kitāb* 'book' (infix *-i-ā-*), etc.

(4) Suprafixes. Here, in a sense, the affix is added "on top of" the stem. Compare the following forms from the Congo language Ngbaka (here *à* etc. denotes low tone, *ā* mid tone, *á* high tone):

Present	*Past*	*Future*	*Imperative*	*Meaning*
yòlò	yōlō	yòló	yóló	'to stand'
b'ìlì	b'īlī	b'ìlí	b'ílí	'to cut'
sà	sā	sàá	sá	'to call'
wà	wā	wàá	wá	'to clean'

Here the suprafix of the present is low tone; the suprafix of the past is mid tone; the suprafix of the future is low tone plus high tone (and a single vowel is doubled to carry both tones); and the suprafix of the imperative is high tone. (This example is adapted from the excellent book by Eugene A. Nida, *Learning a Foreign Language: A Handbook for Missionaries,* New York 1950, p. 161.) In English we use derivational stress suprafixes in such words as: *the óverflòw, the úndertàker* (stress suprafix '+`); *to òverflów, to ùndertáke* (stress suprafix `+'); etc.

A special way of forming affixes (prefixes, infixes, suffixes) is REDUPLICATION, where the phonemic shape of the affix is determined in whole or in part by the phonemic shape of the stem. Classical Greek offers good examples: stem *lū-* 'to loose,' perfect *léluka* 'I have loosed'; stem *graph-* 'to write,' perfect *gégrapha* 'I have written'; stem *paideu-* 'to educate,' perfect *pepáideuka* 'I have educated.' Here we may say that the perfect prefixes *le-, ge-, pe-* have the shape *Ce-,* that is, they consist of the first consonant ("C") of the stem plus the vowel *e.* Ilocano shows an interesting combination of reduplication and infixation. Reduplicative prefixation of the shape CVC- (consonant, vowel, consonant) is first applied to the stem, changing *panaw* to *panpanaw,* and *balay* to *balbalay;* then the infixes *-um-* and *-imm-* are inserted before the first vowel of the now reduplicated stems, giving *pumanpanaw* 'he is going,' *pimmanpanaw* 'he was going,' *bumalbalay* 'he is building a house,' *bimmalbalay* 'he was building a house.'

To give the inflectional PARADIGM of a stem, it is customary to list the stem and its various inflected forms in some conventional order. For example: *boy, boy's, boys, boys';* or *look, looks, looked, looking.* When we apply this procedure to a whole class of words, such as English nouns, we often run into the type of trouble already discussed in Chapter 3: *man, man's, men, men's.* At the grammatical level we assume that *men* consist of "man + 'noun plural'." But at the phonological level this has been encoded into the sequence *men* and we are therefore no longer able to identify the phonemic shape of either the stem or the affix; they have been "fused." In terms of the phonological process involved it is customary to describe this as a fifth type of affixation, namely:

(5) Replacement. We may say that the phonological encoding of "*man* + 'noun plural' " is accomplished by replacing the vowel of

the stem, thereby changing *man* to *men*. Many English verbs show similar "replacive affixes": *take—took, break—broke,* etc. Because such formations are often highly unsystematic, they constitute a heavy learning problem for the student; and the worst of it is that there is nothing that can be done about them. They are simply there, and they have to be learned blindly.

A final type of phonological process which shows up in inflectional paradigms is, fortunately, quite simple to learn:

(6) Subtraction. The classic example is French adjectives. A few examples:

	Masculine		*Feminine*		*Meaning*
(1)	/pəti/	petit	/pətit/	petite	'little'
(2)	/grã/	grand	/grãd/	grande	'big'
(3)	/lɔ̃/	long	/lɔ̃g/	longue	'long'
(4)	/ba/	bas	/bas/	basse	'low'
(5)	/blã/	blanc	/blãš/	blanche	'white'
(6)	/frãsɛ/	français	/frãsɛz/	française	'French'

There are two ways of learning forms of this sort. One is to take the masculine as basic and then to memorize rules for deriving the feminine from the masculine. You must then learn those cases in which /t/ is added, as in (1); those in which /d/ is added, as in (2); those in which /g/ is added, as in (3); those in which /s/ is added, as in (4); those in which /š/ is added, as in (5); those in which /z/ is added, as in (6); etc. Fortunately there is an easier way of handling such forms. Instead of taking the masculine as basic, take the feminine. Then a single general rule will cover all these cases (and scores of others like them): "The masculine is derived from the feminine by subtraction of the final consonant." (The general principle of subtraction applies very well to a large class of French adjectives, though there are complications. Fortunately, there is also a large class of French adjectives in which masculine and feminine are identical.)

In the preceding paragraphs we have discussed the "internal" structure of words; we now need to add a few remarks about what might be called their "external" structure, that is, their phonological shapes in relation to what comes before and after them. First, the language you are studying may have a class (usually small) of words which "lean on" preceding or following words and which are therefore called CLITICS (from Greek *klitikós* 'leaning'). Unstressed English *a* and *an* typically "lean on" a following word (*a head, an ounce,* phonologically just like *ahead, announce*) and are therefore PROCLITICS. Unstressed English *me, us* typically "lean on" a preceding word (*pay me, serve us,* rhyming with *Mamie, nervous*) and are therefore ENCLITICS.

Second, in the language you are learning you may find that the phonemic shapes of words vary depending on the phonemic shapes of the words which precede or follow. In English this can go to extreme lengths, as when the words *miss* /mís/ and *you* /yǘ/ are fused into the single phonological unit (*we're going to*) *miss you* /míšū/ (rhyming with *issue*). Compare also *raise you* /rḙžū/, *hit you* /híčū/, *did you* /díjū/, etc. (In general, the sequences /-s y- -z y- -t y- -d y-/ become /-š- -ž- -č- -ǰ-/, respectively.) This phenomenon is called SANDHI (pronounced *sundy*)—a word borrowed from the old Hindu grammarians and originally meaning 'put together.'

Though we seldom learn about it in school (if it is mentioned at all, we are usually told to avoid it), ordinary spoken American English shows a remarkable amount of sandhi, especially in its various clitics. Consider the following:

Watch out, or it'll fall on		How much will they		
top of me	/tápəmī/	give me	/gímī/	Bess's here.
top of you	/tápəyə/	give you	/gívyə/	/bésiz/
top of him	/tápəvim/	give him	/gívim/	Jack's here.
top of her	/tápəvər/	give her	/gívər/	/ǰǽks/
top of us	/tápəvəs/	give us	/gívəs/	Bob's here.
top of them	/tápəvəm/	give them	/gívəm/	/bábz/

In the third column we again find the familiar phonological rule: /iz/ after sibilants (*Bess's here, Rose's here, Butch's here, George's here*), /s/ after other voiceless phonemes (*Jack's here, Nat's here, Flip's here*), /z/ after other voiced phonemes (*Bob's here, Jim's here, Joe's here*). These are the sandhi forms of enclitic *is*. Interestingly enough, they are also the sandhi forms of enclitic *has: Bess's done it, Jack's done it, Bob's done it*, etc. Some of the sandhi forms of English clitics are reproduced in normal spelling: *I'll* (= both *I shall* and *I will*), *I've, I'd, I'm, you're, he's, isn't, aren't, can't, won't*, etc. Others are not normally written but are just as real nonetheless: *Jack and Jill* /jǽkə̭n jíl/, *head or tails* /hédər tḗlz/, *tea for two* /tīfər tū̃/, *I can fly* /áikən flái/, etc. The reader can perhaps amuse himself by looking for further examples. They involve largely pronouns, auxiliary verbs, some prepositions, some conjunctions.

Sandhi alternations are not necessarily limited to clitics. In certain varieties of English (in eastern New England, for example), such words as *mother, father, Cuba, Russia* all end in the phoneme /ə/ if they stand before pause or before a word beginning with a consonant: /mə́ðə/, /fáðə/, /kyū́bə/, /rə́šə/. If the following word begins with a vowel, however, a so-called "linking *r*" is added between the two words. This then gives *father insists* /fáðə-r-insísts̩/, *mother insists* /mə́ðə-r-insísts/, and also *Cuba insists* /kyū́bə-r-insísts/ and *Russia insists* /rə́šə-r-insísts/.

French shows extensive sandhi involving words of many types. The numeral *six* 'six' is /si/ before consonants: /sifam/ *six femmes* 'six women,' but it is /siz/ before vowels: /sizɔm/ *six hommes* 'six men,' and it is /sis/ before pause or in counting; the word *dix* 'ten' behaves similarly. Sometimes the sandhi varies depending on the grammatical structure. The word /savã/ *savant* is both a noun 'scholar' and an adjective 'learned'; and the word /etrãže/ *étranger* is both a noun 'foreigner' and an adjective 'foreign.' In the construction NOUN + ADJECTIVE, *savant* has its normal shape: /ɛ̃ savã etrãže/ *un savant étranger* 'a foreign scholar'; but in the construction ADJECTIVE + NOUN it has a special sandhi shape: /ɛ̃ savã-t-etrãže/ *un savant étranger* 'a learned foreigner.'

Dutch shows a highly regular type of sandhi involving the voiceless consonants /p t f s/ and the corresponding voiced consonants /b d v z/. Across word boundaries, any sequence of these phonemes must be either all voiceless or all voiced; and if the application of the sandhi rules gives two successive occurrences of the same phoneme, these are collapsed into one. Compare the following, in which *vier, vijf, zes* mean 'four, five, six,' and *bomen, dagen, zakken, voeten* mean 'trees, days, sacks, feet,' respectively:

(1) vier bomen	/vīr bṓmə/	vier dagen	/vīr dāɣə/
(2) vijf bomen	/veiv bṓmə/	vijf dagen	/veiv dāɣə/
(3) zes bomen	/zez bṓmə/	zes dagen	/zez dāɣə/
(4) vier zakken	/vīr zakə/	vier voeten	/vīr vutə/

(5) vijf zakken /veif sakə/   vijf voeten /vei-f-utə/
(6) zes zakken /ze-s-akə/   zes voeten /zes futə/

When spoken in isolation, the three numerals have the phonemic shapes /vīr veif zes/ and the four nouns have the phonemic shapes /bōmə dāɣə zakə vutə/. Rows (2) and (3) show that final /-f/ and /-s/ are voiced to /-v/ and /-z/ before a following voiced /b-/ or /d-/. Rows (5) and (6) show that initial /z-/ and /v-/ are unvoiced to /s-/ and /f-/ after a preceding voiceless /-f/ or /-s/. And the second column of row (5) and the first column of row (6) show how the resulting clusters /-f f-/ and /-s s-/ are simplified to /-f-/ and /-s-/.

Though Dutch sandhi may appear at first glance to be quite formidable, it actually poses no great learning problem because it is entirely regular. One simply gets in the habit of pronouncing sequences of consonants across word boundaries as all-voiceless or all-voiced; and our English pronunciation habits make it easy to shorten theoretical /-f f-/ and /-s s-/ to simple /-f-/ and /-s-/. More difficult is French sandhi, since it involves matters of grammar as well as of phonology. Still more difficult is English sandhi, because the phonological shapes of words can be altered so drastically. When we, as native speakers, hear the phoneme sequence /áidə wónə •gṓ/, we may at first decode it as a nonsensical *Ida wanna go*. But we know the code so well that its redundancy allows us to build this up successively into /ái dónt wóntə •gṓ/ and then into the theoretical (but hardly ever pronounced) sequence of full forms: /ái dū́ nát wónt tū́ •gṓ/ *I do not want to go*. This is where the foreign learner gets into trouble; this is one of the reasons why, as we have already noted, he finds it so hard to follow a conversation in a noisy restaurant or to talk over the telephone. Understanding any language, as it is normally spoken, involves constant referrals from the phonological code to the grammatical code to the semantic code and out into the speech situation. A foreigner can eventually learn to do this as well as a native speaker, but it takes a lot of practice.

Chapter Seven

Meaning

Meaning is a topic which only the most foolhardy would attempt to discuss in a book like the present one. Philosophers have struggled with the concept "meaning" for centuries, and even today there is not full agreement as to what "meaning" really means. And yet, in a book on learning foreign languages, we simply *must* discuss this topic, because the very essence of language is the correlation between sound on the one hand and meaning on the other. Our learning of meaning begins when we are babies, and adults start waving objects in front of our faces and making noises at the same time ("Dolly! Dolly! See the dolly!"), hoping that we will get the connection between sound and meaning and thereby learn a bit of language. We learn more meaning (grammatical meaning this time) as we catch on to the fact that our language says "Mama loves baby" vs. "Baby loves Mama." We continue learning meaning by making use of the marvelous redundancy which our language contains— allowing us to learn most of the words we know *not* by having objects waved in our faces, *not* by having explanations given to us, and *not* by looking words up in a dictionary, but by observing (mostly quite unconsciously) the contexts in which the words occur. Though we learn the basic structure of our language by the time we are five or six, we continue learning new words—and new meanings—all our lives.

When most of us think of "meaning," we think primarily of the way we use words as labels for things in the world about us. "Meaning" here lies in our association of the sound of a word with

101

the object which it denotes. The compulsion to use words as labels in this way is remarkably strong in us. When someone shows us a flower which we do not know, the first thing we ask is what its "name" is—even though we may not be particularly interested in flowers and never really intend to use the name again. It somehow bothers us to have a bit of the world called to our attention and not to have a label which we can attach to it. Scientists behave in just the same way: as soon as they have identified some new item in their science, they either make up a name for it themselves or else run to a colleague in the Classics Department and ask him to suggest a proper Greek or Latin term.

Much of meaning also lies within the grammar of our language. Words strung along in a row cannot produce a meaningful message unless they are arranged in one of the ways provided for by the grammar of our language. We may recall again how much of *Jabberwocky* we were able to understand, despite the fact that so many of the words denoted nothing at all. (As Alice said: "Somehow it seems to fill my head with ideas—only I don't exactly know what they are!") We may also recall that the so-called "function words" often carry little more than grammatical meaning. Yet they are from one point of view the most important words of all and the ones which we must try to learn right from the start.

Still another aspect of "meaning" lies within us, the individual speakers of the language. We can call one and the same object the "Evening Star" at seven o'clock in the evening but the "Morning Star" twelve hours later, and not be bothered by the fact that the object denoted is in each case the same. As we grow up, our ideas as to the "meaning" of such words as *truth* and *beauty*, or *heat* and *light*, may change drastically, even though the labels themselves remain the same.

In the following paragraphs we shall discuss these three aspects of meaning as they affect the foreign language learner: (1) meaning and things, often called "denotative meaning"; (2) meaning and grammar, often called "grammatical meaning"; and (3) meaning and people, often called "connotative meaning."

Meaning and things. Perhaps the most common misconception about meaning is the belief that the world in which we live consists of a certain number of "things," and that each language simply attaches to these things its own particular labels. What is in English a *house* is in French a *maison,* in Spanish a *casa,* in German a *Haus,* in Russian a *dom,* in Ilocano a *balay,* etc. It is hard to know where this idea originated. Perhaps the first statement of it is that in the Book of Genesis, where God "called the light Day, . . . the darkness . . . Night, . . . the firmament Heaven, . . . the dry land Earth, . . . the gathering together of the waters . . . Seas" (Genesis 1:5-10), and where "Adam gave names to all cattle, and to the fowl of the air, and to every beast of the field" (Genesis 2:20). If the world really *did* consist of a specific number of objects to which, after Babel, each language attached its own particular linguistic symbols, then learning a foreign language would consist largely of learning new labels for old things. As we saw in Chapter 3, however, this is clearly *not* the way in which languages work. Even if someone *could* tell us how many colors there are in the spectrum, each language would go on looking at the spectrum in its own particular way.

Perhaps the most fundamental fact which we should realize about words and their denotative meanings is that the connection between the two is arbitrary, and that it is arbitrary in two different respects. First of all, even if we suppose that there exists in the world some such necessary entity as "dog," it is totally arbitrary that this should be symbolized by the sounds *dog* in English, *chien* in French, *perro* in Spanish, *cane* in Italian, *Hund* in German, *sobá-ka* in Russian, and so on. If we ask "why" any one of these languages uses its particular word, we can give an explanation of sorts: French says *chien* and Italian says *cane* because the Romans said (in the accusative) *canem,* and these are the modern French and Italian developments of this 2500-year-old form. In like manner, we could try to find older forms of the word for dog in the other languages. This "explains" the modern forms in a certain sense; but in effect it simply pushes the real explanation back some twenty centuries or more in time since now we must again ask: why did the Romans call a dog (in the accusative) a *canem?* Perhaps it would be more accurate, however, to say that such historical "explanations" really circumvent the question we are asking. I myself call a dog a *dog* not because I know anything about the history of this form, but simply because everybody else in my language calls a dog a *dog.* If, when I was learning English, everybody had called it a *wug,* I would have used this set of noises instead. Just which set of noises we use in a language is quite arbitrary; the only important thing is that we all use the *same* set of noises, since otherwise the language will not work.

For whatever reason, many people find it very difficult to accept the notion that there is no logical connection between the sound of a word and the thing it refers to. Since the evidence seems to be irrefutable, they usually swallow hard and try to accept it. But then they inevitably come up with one apparent exception. How about onomatopoetic words, such as *bowwow* for the noise which a dog makes when he barks? Surely the connection here is not arbitrary! Indeed it is not (entirely) arbitrary. This is why we recognize a special class of onomatopoetic words in the first place—precisely because in this respect such words are abnormal. The very fact that we set up such a special class shows clearly that, in the normal case, the connection between sound and meaning *is* totally arbitrary. Even in the case of onomatopoetic words the connection is not as "logical" as we usually think it is. Instead of *bowwow,* a Japanese dog says *wan-wan* ("wong-wong")—and this is hardly what we, as speakers of English, would have expected from the onomatopoetic theory of a "natural" connection between sound and meaning. Here, too, there is much more arbitrariness than we might have expected. The learner can amuse and instruct himself by finding out some of the onomatopoetic words in the language he is learning.

The second respect in which the connection between a word and its meaning is arbitrary concerns the area of reality to which it refers. It is quite arbitrary that such a bit of reality should be referred to by one word rather than by two or more—or, indeed, that it should be referred to by any word at all. Since we have in English such terms as *ear lobe, cheek, jowls,* and the like, why don't we have any name for that bit of skin which connects the base of the thumb and the base of the forefinger? Since we have a name for a closed hand (a *fist*), why don't we have any name for an open hand? If a *lap* is the area formed when we bend our legs more or less at right angles to our trunk, why don't we have a name for the area formed when we bend our forearms more or less at right angles to our trunk—the area we use when we bring in some logs of wood for the fire? By and large it seems that any language has words for those items in the culture which are important to its speakers. The classic example always cited is Eskimo, with its half a dozen or more words for different types of snow. An example closer to home is the language of carpenters. Anyone who has ever had a house built, and has talked with the carpenters as it went up, will have heard all sorts of unfamiliar labels which he himself never knew before and never felt a need for—because he is not a carpenter. Whenever a need for new words *does* arise, every language seems to be able to create them—either by borrowing them from some other language (*sputnik*) or by making them out of native materials (*spacesuit*) or foreign materials (*astronaut*). We even have words for things which have never existed in the past and will never exist in the future, such as *unicorn* and *dragon*.

As one example of the arbitrary way in which we combine bits and pieces of reality into units by means of the words which we attach to them, consider the following example from English. We group together a vast array of different objects into a single semantic unit through the label *stool*. The objects may be of wood or of metal, have three or four legs, and be short or tall, plain or upholstered, and of any color at all. As soon as we add a back, however, we get a different semantic unit: a *chair*. And as soon as we widen the object so that two or more people can sit on it, we get still another semantic unit: a *bench*. If to a chair we add upholstery, its semantic allegiance does not change: it is still a *chair*. But if to a bench we add upholstery, it becomes quite a different semantic unit: a *sofa*. All of this is highly arbitrary, and we cannot expect that any other language—through its words—will group things together in just this same way.

Some idea of the way different languages structure the world about us through the labels they attach to it can be gained by considering how a number of them use their demonstratives to structure the continuum of space. French lumps all of space into its single demonstrative *ce: ce livre* 'this/that book.' (If a further structuring of space is desired, it has to be accomplished by adding the enclitics *-ci* 'here' and *-là* 'there': *ce livre-ci, ce livre-là*.) English divides all of space into just two segments: *this book* (near the speaker), *that book* (somewhere else). Russian makes a similar division: *éta kn'íga, tá kn'íga;* but *éta* covers a larger amount of space than English *this,* and *tá* covers a correspondingly smaller amount than English *that*. Spanish carves space into three areas: *este libro* (near the speaker), *ese libro* (near the listener), *aquel libro* (elsewhere). (This is true, at least, of space in Spain; but in Spanish America *ese* generally usurps the area of *aquel*.) Ilocano structures space (plus a bit of time) into no less than five different segments: *tuy libru* (near the speaker), *ta libru* (near the listener), *dyay libru* (away from both), *tay libru* (out of sight), and *di libru* (no longer existing).

In talking about space, or the color spectrum, one might object that we are dealing in each case with a continuum, so that no two languages could even be expected to carve it up in just the same way. Let us therefore look at an area of reality which has a precise and verifiable structure: family relationships. In the normal case it is easy to determine with complete exactitude whether one man is or is not another man's father, son, uncle, cousin, nephew, etc. Precisely because this area of reality is so easy to handle, it has long been a favorite subject of study by anthropologists: they have been interested in the light which kinship terms can throw on patterns of family relationship. It has not only been extensively investigated; it has become a classic example of how *differently* various languages, through the words they use, carve up one and the same area of reality. We think of a *brother* as any male child by the same parents as ours; many languages have no word for this, but only for *older brother* or *younger brother*. Though we have words combining male and female in direct line of descent one generation above us (*parent*) and one generation below us (*child*), in our own generation we have only the rare word *sibling* and usually use instead of this the words *brother* and *sister,* which then require us to specify sex. We again insist on specifying sex in the case of 'child of my aunt and uncle,' namely *nephew* vs. *niece;* but if we want to state such a person's relationship to ourselves, we can *not* specify sex but can say only *cousin.* Dutch does the opposite: one and the same word for *nephew/niece* and *cousin,* though sex must be specified: *neef* 'nephew, male cousin,' *nicht* 'niece, female cousin.' We have the words *aunt* and *uncle,* but we have no word to distinguish whether they are brother/sister of our father or brother/sister of our mother; and we have no single term which combines both sexes (parallel to *child, parent*). Furthermore, we commonly use *aunt* and *uncle* to refer to persons who stand in no blood relationship to us whatever. For the parents of our parents, we have the combined term *grandparents* and the separate terms *grandfather* and *grandmother*; but we do not have terms to distinguish the parents of our mother from the parents of our father. When A's son marries B's daughter, we have terms for the new relationship of the daughter to A (*daughter-in-law*) and of the son to B (*son-in-law*), but we have no term for the new relationship of A to B.

The point has been made, and we need go no further. Metaphorically speaking, every language slices the pie of reality in its own whimsical way. When we learn a new language, we must remember this and not be surprised that it looks at the world, through its words, in a way that is very different from that of English.

Meaning and grammar. Many times in the previous chapters we have had occasion to speak of "grammatical meanings" of various sorts. There is for instance the meaning "completion" which we signal by using the terminal intonations /↓/ and /↑/: "It's raining." vs. "It's raining?" The latter also contains the meaning "please answer yes or no," and this meaning may be further reinforced by using a different word order: "Is it raining?" There is the meaning "command to perform such and such an action" which we arrive at by transforming "You will work hard" to "Work hard." There is what might be called the "equational meaning" which we signal by using the structure "X is Y." We subdivide this into two types depending on whether we select for the slot "Y" a noun: *The man is a doctor,* or an adjective: *The man is sick.* If the latter, we can transform this into a meaning of "attribution": *the sick man.* Every construction has its own constructional meaning.

Much of the grammatical meaning which we derive from any sentence comes not from its SURFACE STRUCTURE but rather from the DEEP STRUCTURE which lies beneath the surface. Consider such a sentence as: *The man was upset by the boy's being accused of cheating.* On the surface, *the man* is the subject of *was upset,* and *the boy's* is a modifier of *being accused of cheating.* Semantically, however, we interpret *the man* as the object of *upset,* and *the boy* as simultaneously the object of *accuse* and the subject of *cheat.* How are we to explain this apparent discrepancy between grammatical structure and semantic interpretation? The theory of transformational grammar explains it by making the following assumptions:

(1) The grammatical code provides for two levels of structure:

(a) At the "deep" level, it produces the structures which underlie the simple sentences (*Something*) *upset the man,* (*Someone*) *accused the boy of (something), The boy cheated.*

(b) At the "surface" level, it produces by transformation the structure which underlies the derived sentence *The man was upset by the boy's being accused of cheating.*

(2) The semantic code takes the deep structure and from it produces the semantic interpretation which we give to the sentence—that is, the way we understand it.

(3) The phonological code takes the surface structure and from it produces the phonological interpretation which we give to the sentence—that is, the way we say it.

These assumptions now make it quite clear why we can view the forms *the man* and *the boy* in such different ways. *The man* is the subject of *was upset* because this is its status in the surface structure *The man was upset* . . .; but we understand it as the object of *upset* because this is its status in the deep structure (*Something*) *upset the man.* Similarly, *the boy* (with *'s* added) is the modifier of *being accused of cheating* because this is its status in the surface structure *the boy's being accused of cheating;* but we understand it as the object of *accuse* and the subject of *cheat* because this is its status in the deep structures (*Someone*) *accused the boy of* (*something*) and *The boy cheated.*

Of particular interest to the foreign language learner are the COMPULSORY GRAMMATICAL CATEGORIES which he may find in the language he is studying. These are meanings which the grammar of the language forces us to signal whether we want to or not. Though it is impossible to give a full list, there are at least ten general types which are common enough so that the learner should be alerted to the fact that he may find one or more of them in his language.

(1) Number. This includes singular/plural, sometimes singular/ dual/plural, rarely singular/dual/trial/plural. The categories singular/plural are familiar to us from English. They are compulsory in nearly all our nouns: *man/men, dog/dogs,* etc.; in some of our pronouns: *he/they* etc.; in two noun modifiers: *this/these, that/ those;* and in the present tense agreement between subject and verb: *the dog bites/the dogs bite.* Interestingly enough, this present tense agreement shows up even with those nouns which do not themselves show the singular/plural categories: *the sheep is/the sheep are.*

(2) Gender. Here a great deal of confusion is caused by the terms (familiar from Latin) *masculine, feminine,* and *neuter.* The word *gender* itself has no necessary connection with sex, but simply means 'kind,' 'type,' 'sort.' (It comes from Latin *genus, generis.*) The terms *masculine* and *feminine* were originally used, in languages which have this classification, only because one grammatical class of nouns happened to contain (among many others) most words denoting male beings of various sorts, and another class happened to contain (among many others) most words denoting female beings of various sorts; and then, if there was a third class, it was dubbed "neither" (Latin *neuter*). Though the French noun *la table* 'the table' belongs to the same (feminine) gender as *la femme* 'the woman,' the French do not in any sense think of a table as somehow "female"; and though the German noun *das Mädchen* 'the girl' belongs to the same (neuter) gender as *das Buch* 'the book,' the Germans most decidedly do not think of girls as being sexless. These are purely grammatical classes, and they have no necessary connection with the world outside of grammar. (Because the traditional terms *masculine, feminine, neuter* are so misleading, one almost wishes they could be replaced by *red, white, blue,* or *Republican, Democratic, Socialist.* These terms would do just as well, and they would have the great advantage that no one would take them seriously.)

The gender of English nouns shows up mainly in the selection of noun-substitutes. The primary categories are "personal/impersonal"; within the former there are the secondary categories "masculine/feminine." Examples: (1) personal, (1a) masculine *the man —he,* (1b) feminine *the woman—she;* (2) impersonal *the table—it.* All gender categories are suspended in the plural: *the men, the women, the tables—they.* The personal/impersonal categories also show up in question words: *who did it* vs. *what did it.* The system is by no means consistent, since we may have: *the baby—he, she, it; the ship—it, she; the auto—it, she (Fill her up!);* etc. Furthermore, since the "personal" category may include large numbers of living beings other than people (*the dog—he, the cat—she*), the primary classification comes close to the type which is better labeled "animate/inanimate" rather than "personal/impersonal."

The language you are learning may show no such gender categories, or it may show as many as half a dozen of them. The categories may appear in noun-substitutes, in noun-modifiers, in the forms of the nouns themselves, in gender agreement between noun-subject and verb, in gender agreement between noun-object and verb—or in any combination of these plus perhaps some others. French shows the categories "masculine/feminine," and these appear in both singular and plural in noun-substitutes and in many noun-modifiers; and they appear to some extent in the forms of the nouns, in agreement between noun-subject and verb, and in agreement between noun-object and verb. Dutch shows the categories "common/neuter," and within the "common" gender there is a partial subclassification into "masculine/feminine." All Dutch gender categories are suspended in the plural, however. German and Russian show the three categories "masculine/feminine/neuter." Many American Indian languages (among others) show the classification "animate/inanimate"; as in English, the animate class then generally includes a few nouns which do not actually denote animate objects. Some languages of Africa show six genders, and the categories appear in grammatical agreement between noun and noun-modifier, noun-subject and verb, and noun-object and verb.

(3) Case. The fragments of a case system which we have in English are highly irregular in shape and appear only in some of the pronouns: subjective *I, he, she, we, they, who;* objective *me, him, her, us, them, whom.* (Instead of "subjective" and "objective" one could use other names.) Something close to a case appears in the English "possessive": *the man's,* though it is unusual in that this suffix can be attached to whole noun phrases: *my brother-in-law's house, the Queen of England's hat.* German has four cases, customarily called nominative, accusative, dative, genitive. Its cases are more commonly signaled in noun-modifiers than in the shapes of the nouns themselves: nominative *der Mann kommt* 'the man is coming,' accusative *ich sehe den Mann* 'I see the man,' dative *mit dem Mann* 'with the man' (though very formally this can be marked as dative by use of the affix *-e: mit dem Manne*); the only case consistently marked in this type of noun is the genitive: *der Sohn des Mannes* 'the son of the man.' Latin has five cases (plus fragments of a few others): nominative *urbs* 'city,' genitive *urbis,* dative *urbī,* accusative *urbem,* ablative *urbe;* in the plural, however, nominative and accusative often have the same shape, and the dative and ablative of the

plural *always* have the same shape. Other languages may show up to a score or so of cases. If there are large numbers of them, they are likely to be formed quite regularly.

(4) Definiteness. English signals the categories "definite/indefinite" syntactically, by means of words: definite *the man,* indefinite *a man.* Other languages signal it morphologically, by means of affixes; and the affixes may be either prefixes or, as in Rumanian and the Scandinavian languages, suffixes. Somewhat similar to the categories "definite/indefinite" are those which we have in English "count nouns" and "mass nouns": count noun *a pencil, some pencils;* mass noun *milk, some milk.* Many nouns have different semantic denotations depending on which way they are used: count noun *a paper, some papers* vs. mass noun *paper, some paper.*

(5) Size and shape. Japanese (to name just one example) uses special morphemes ("counters") with its numerals depending on the size, shape, etc. of the things being counted. Four such counters are:

Plain numeral		Used with Counter 1	Used with Counter 2	Used with Counter 3	Used with Counter 4
iti	'1'	iti-mai	iti-dai	is-satu	ip-poñ
ni	'2'	ni-mai	ni-dai	ni-satu	ni-hoñ
sañ	'3'	sañ-mai	sañ-dai	sañ-satu	sañ-boñ
si/yoñ	'4'	yoñ-mai	yoñ-dai	yoñ-satu	yoñ-hoñ
go	'5'	go-mai	go-dai	go-satu	go-hoñ

Counter 1 is used in counting thin, flat objects: sheets, blankets, plates, boards, rugs, leaves, etc. Counter 2 is used in counting vehicles: autos, busses, carriages, carts, etc. Counter 3 is used in counting bound volumes: books, magazines, albums, etc. Counter 4 is used in counting long, cylindrical objects: pens, pencils, arms, legs, trecs, poles, etc.

(6) Person. English has the categories "1st person," singular *I,* plural *we;* "2nd person" *you* (with no distinction between singular and plural, though Biblical English still has singular *thou,* plural *ye);* "3rd person," singular *he* (personal-masculine), *she* (personal-feminine), *it* (impersonal), plural *they.* You may find that the language you are learning distinguishes between an "inclusive 1st person plural" (speaker and hearer and perhaps others) and an

"exclusive 1st person plural" (speaker and others, but not hearer). It may also distinguish between an "inclusive 2nd person plural" (hearer(s) and others not present) and an "exclusive 2nd person plural" (hearers, but no others). Or it may have a so-called "4th person," to distinguish between the first and second of two persons mentioned other than speaker and hearer: "Did *I* (1st person) tell *you* (2nd person) that I saw *Bill* (3rd person) talking to *Tom* (4th person)? *He* (to be marked either 3rd or 4th) will give *him* (to be marked either 4th or 3rd) the money tomorrow." Such categories of person show up perhaps universally in pronouns. They may also appear in agreement between noun-subject and verb (compare *I see* but *he, she, it sees*), perhaps also in agreement between verb and noun-object.

(7) Tense. Common categories are: present, past, future, pre-past ("pluperfect"), pre-future ("future perfect"). In English we are forced to distinguish morphologically between present and past: *I see* vs. *I saw.* We can also distinguish syntactically (using phrases) between future *I shall/will see,* pre-past *I had seen,* pre-future *I shall/will have seen.* Notice that our so-called "present" is in a sense also timeless: "Water *boils* at 100° centigrade." The language you are learning may have a special form for this.

(8) Aspect. Categories of this type have to do with whether an action is looked upon as complete or incomplete, as occurring at one point in time or over a stretch of time, as occurring only once or repetitively or habitually, and the like. English has an interesting compulsory distinction between "past without present relevance" (*I worked here for ten years,* implying that I no longer do) and "past with present relevance" (*I have worked here for ten years,* implying that I still do). English also distinguishes between "punctual," referring to a point in time (*I worked in Chicago*), and "durative," referring to a stretch of time (*I was working in Chicago*).

(9) Mood. Categories of this type refer to the speaker's attitude toward an action. A language may distinguish between such things as a neutral attitude (often called "indicative"), an attitude which has certain reservations ("subjunctive"), an attitude of hope ("optative"), an attitude of doubt ("dubitative"), an attitude of possibility ("potential"), an attitude of desire ("desiderative"), an attitude of unreality ("unreal"), an attitude of negativeness ("negative"), an at-

titude of questioning ("interrogative"), an attitude of emphasis ("emphatic"), an attitude of condition ("conditional"), and the like. English has a sort of optative in its use of an uninflected verb form with a 3rd person singular subject: "I insist that he *live* in a dormitory" (vs. the indicative "I insist that he *lives* in a dormitory"); and it has one verb with a special unreal form, namely the use of *were* with a singular subject: "if he *were* here" (implying that he is not; though many of us also say "if he *was* here"). Aside from this, the closest we come to "moods" is through our use of normal verb forms in special contexts. We can produce something close to an "unreal" mood by using a past tense form in a present tense context: "if I *had* the money today"; something close to a "conditional" by using past *would* in a present tense context: "I *would* buy a hat" (this use is actually far commoner than the past tense use of *would*, which occurs in such sentences as: "he *would* always stutter when he tried to say it"); and something close to an "emphatic" mood by using *do/did* in contexts where otherwise the present or past of a full verb is used: "but he *does* live here," "but he *did* pay the bill."

(10) Voice. Categories of this type refer to the grammatical relationships between a verbal expression and the nominal expressions which are in construction with it. In English *The policeman shot the man* the policeman is the doer of the action and the man is the person affected by it; in *The man was shot by the policeman* the same relationships are expressed in a grammatically different way. The former grammatical structure is customarily called "active," the latter "passive." In English the active is expressed by a word (*shot*), the passive by a phrase (*was shot*); in the language you are learning the passive may be indicated by an affix attached to the verb stem. Other types of voice include: reflexive (the subject acting upon itself), reciprocal (the subjects acting upon each other), causitive (the subject causing an action to happen), transitive (an action involving an object), intransitive (an action not involving an object). The language you are learning may indicate one or more such voices by means of affixes.

Meaning and people. We have seen that "meaning" lies partly in the connection between a word and its referent (denotative meaning), and partly within the grammar of the language (grammatical meaning); to a remarkable extent it also lies within people as users of a language (connotative meaning). To illustrate this, try the following experiment: ask a number of speakers of English what the word *livid* means to them. Answers may range all the way from 'pale' through 'bluish' to 'red.' Since most of us use the word only in such contexts as *livid with rage,* perhaps its common denotative meaning can be phrased as "denoting whatever color the user associates with extreme anger." The word is unusual in that different people associate it with such different colors. By and large we cannot allow the words of a language to behave in this way. There must in general be a kind of tacit agreement among all speakers of a language that such connotative meanings shall not cover so wide an area; otherwise language would be a very poor means of communication. Needless to say, our disagreements as to the meaning of *livid* would soon disappear if we began using it in such contexts as "Please show me a *livid* dress."

Though the word *livid* is an extreme case, many—perhaps most—content words show some such fluctuation from speaker to speaker, or from one group to another. A woman whom men call *pretty* is likely to look quite different from a woman whom women call *pretty.* The connotative meaning which a word carries for us seems to be a compounding of all the contexts—both linguistic and non-linguistic—in which we have encountered it. This leads to various groupings of words, some of which may be shared by all speakers and some of which may be quite personal. A personal example: To the writer, such words as *ocean, sea, waves* connote such further words (plus their denotations and connotations) as *happiness, vacation, sunshine, relaxation,* and the like. (This is presumably because, as a boy, he spent many summers at the seashore—and regrets only that he cannot do so as an adult.) To others, such words might connote *shipwreck, disaster, seasickness,* and so on. When such groupings of words are shared more or less by all speakers of a language, they lead to what have been called WORD FIELDS or SEMANTIC FIELDS. Thus the word *good* belongs to a word field which includes *beneficial, valuable, excellent, useful, advantageous, profitable, salutary, healthful,* and the like. This leads to the concept of SYNONYMS: words which are very close in meaning. Interestingly enough, it also leads to the concept of ANTONYMS: words which are opposite in meaning, since we also associate opposites with each other.

The foreign-language learner will find it very difficult to grasp much of the connotative meaning of many words which he learns. The reason is clear: we accumulate most types of connotative meaning only by having experienced a word in many different linguistic. and non-linguistic contexts; and this takes much time. On the other hand, a proper attention to contexts can in other ways be very helpful right from the start. When you learn a word such as *hat,* learn also a group of words which can be used with it in the same context, such as *coat, buy, store, gray, wear;* this will make it easier to carry on little conversations in the foreign language, as part of the learning process. When you learn one color term, learn half a dozen. Also learn antonyms: *good—bad, short—tall, high—low,* etc. At the same time, be reasonable: do not try to learn *all* the terms for articles of clothing which the language uses. And do not, at this time, try to learn endless lists of synonyms; the subtle distinctions between them had best be postponed for later on. When you begin to read, use context in another way: do not look up the meaning of each new word you come to, but make intelligent guesses as to what its meaning must be on the basis of the context in which it occurs. Remember that this is the way you learned most of the words you know in English.

Translation. Before we leave the topic of meaning, a final remark needs to be made about another subject: translation. In the preceding paragraphs we have suggested that no two languages structure the world of reality in the same way, so that their denotative meanings must be different; it is obvious that no two languages have the same grammar, so that their grammatical meanings must be different; and since their speakers have had different linguistic and non-linguistic experiences from our own, the connotative meanings must be even *more* different. If all this is true, then it must be quite impossible to translate a sentence of one language into a sentence of another language. If by "translation" we mean "word-for-word translation," this is quite correct. Even such languages as English and German—closely related and belonging to the same Western European cultural tradition—contain hosts of words which cannot be translated directly from the one language into the other. Many people make a kind of parlor sport out of identifying such words. Favorite examples of untranslatable German words are *gemütlich* (something like 'homey, easygoing, humbly pleasant, informal') and *Schadenfreude* ('pleasure over the fact that someone else has suffered a misfortune'); favorite examples of untranslatable English words are *sophisticated* and *efficient*. Doubtless the reader can add examples of his own from other languages.

A word of caution needs to be added concerning this parlor sport, fascinating as it may be. Far too often, those who indulge in it jump to the conclusion that the lack of word-for-word equivalents implies also the lack of what is denoted by these words. If this were true, we would have to conclude that speakers of English never meet together in a *gemütlich* way and never indulge in *Schadenfreude;* and that there are no *sophisticated* Germans in a country where there is also no *efficiency* in industry. Or, to use a previous example: We would have to conclude that a Russian can't tell his arm from his hand, since he uses the single word *ruká* to include both. But this is obviously absurd. It is perfectly true that none of these words can be translated in an exact, unambiguous way; but it is also true that, as soon as we abandon the primitive notion of word-for-word translation, anything which can be said in one language can be translated more or less accurately into another. A paper on physics or chemistry will cause the least trouble: the international scientific community has labored long and hard over exact denotative meanings; connotative meanings are out of place in a scientific paper; the only difficulties will be those of translating grammatical meanings. A novel will be considerably more difficult, since here we also begin to run into differences of denotative and connotative meaning. Hardest of all will be a poem if, as is so often the case, the poet has purposely used wide ranges of denotative and connotative meaning. Indeed, here one can fairly say: such a poem is untranslatable. The "translation" may be a very fine poem in its own right (it may even be better than the original), but it cannot be the *same* poem. Except in the case of poems, however, reasonably accurate translation between languages is impossible only in those cases where something—most often a cultural institution of some sort—occurs in the one society but not in the other. American examples: *high school, college, drugstore,* and the like—since no other countries have institutions quite like these.

The above remarks lead us to one final conclusion. Translation is a high art, which requires great knowledge and great skill. The beginner who thinks he can indulge in it is suffering from delusions of grandeur.

Chapter Eight

Writing

In discussing writing in its relation to language learning, we must at the very start emphasize a fact that language learners often tend to forget. No ordinary writing system was ever designed to meet the needs of people who are *learning* the language; it was designed only for those who already *know* the language. The implications for the language learner are clear. No one can hope to achieve much success by looking at black marks on paper (the writing) and then trying to make appropriate noises (the language). Instead, he must first learn some of the language and then note how what he has learned happens to be symbolized in writing. Writing is not a set of directions telling us how a language should be pronounced; it is a method of reminding us on paper of things that we already know how to say. Because writing has only this latter purpose, it can—and does—omit many crucial details of the language itself. The great amount of redundancy in language allows the reader to supply most of the missing details—though only if he already knows the language.

Because writing involves the use of symbols, we need to discuss briefly the ways in which symbols work. Consider the following three very different types of symbols: (1) a red-white-and-blue barber pole, outside a barbershop; (2) the written symbol &; (3) the written symbol *cat*. What does each of these symbols denote? What is in each case the referent? In the case of the barber pole, we can say that it denotes "a barbershop," or "a place where men can get their hair cut," or the like. Or, if the person to whom we are trying

117

to explain the meaning does not know English, we need not use language at all. We can simply point to the barber pole and then take him inside and let him see what is going on. As a symbol, then, a barber pole has no LINGUISTIC REFERENCE; it refers directly to the concept "barbershop," and does not do so by the way of language as an intermediary.

What does the written symbol & denote? What is *its* referent? At first we may be inclined to interpret this as the same type of symbol as a barber pole, and to say that it denotes the idea of "coordination," or "addition," or the like. Here, however, we have skipped a step, since these interpretations refer not to the written symbol & but to the spoken word "and." In the case of a barber pole, there are any number of ways we can phrase our explanation: "a barbershop," "an establishment where men get their hair cut," etc. But in the case of & there is only one thing we can say (in English) if we are asked to give its denotation: the spoken word "and." This & is therefore a very different kind of symbol from a barber pole: it has LINGUISTIC REFERENCE. Here *two* levels of symbolization are involved: the written symbol & has (in English) as its referent the spoken symbol "and"; and only this latter has as its referent the idea "coordination," "addition," or the like.

Consider, finally, the written symbol *cat*. Here *three* levels of symbolic structure are involved: (1) each of the letters *c, a, t* is a symbol for a particular phoneme of English; (2) these three phonemes arranged in this order give a second symbol, the spoken word "cat"; (3) this spoken word "cat" is the symbol for the particular animal *Felis domestica* (or however we want to describe it). The written symbol *cat* is therefore quite different from either of the preceding two symbols. Schematically we can indicate these three different types of symbols as follows:

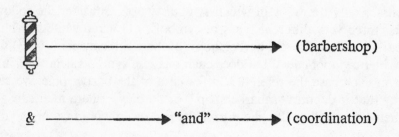

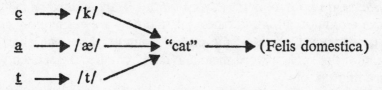

Note particularly the different numbers of symbolic stages involved in symbols of these different types: one in the case of the barber pole, two in the case of &, three in the case of *cat*.

We need to emphasize the differences among these three types of symbols precisely because we have all had years of very useful training in *overlooking* the differences. There was perhaps a time in our lives when, seeing the written symbol &, we first had to "say it out loud" (i.e. give its referent, the spoken word "and") and could only then go on to the final referent "coordination" (or whatever). Now we can skip this intermediate step, and we therefore tend to forget that it even exists. Similarly, there was perhaps a time in our lives when, seeing the written symbolization *cat*, we first had to "sound out" the three letters (i.e. give their referents, the phonemes /k/, /æ/, /t/), then say the spoken word "cat" (composed of these three phonemes in this order), and could only then go on to the final referent *Felis domestica* (or whatever). All of this was necessary if we were to understand the basic nature of our spelling system, which consists of just these three steps. As soon as we had grasped this basic nature, however, our teachers quite properly trained us to omit the intermediate steps. They trained us first not to "sound out" the letters of each word but to read it aloud as a whole, thus omitting the first step; and then they trained us to omit the second step by reading silently. It was splendid that they should have taught us this, since only in this way can we read with useful speed. The only disadvantage is that, after years of practice in omitting the intermediate steps, we now tend to forget that they even exist. Yet they *do* exist, and we must realize this clearly when we come to examine the types of writing systems used in the languages of the world.

All writing systems used for natural languages fall (often with a great many inconsistencies) into two basic types. First, there are those in which the written symbols refer not to sounds but (like English &, +, —, ×, ÷, %, *1, 2, 3*, etc.) directly to WORDS. Such systems are LOGOGRAPHIC ("word writing"), the individual symbols have MORPHOLOGICAL REFERENCE, and they are customarily called CHARACTERS. Chinese is the classic example: here one character denotes the spoken word meaning 'man,' another the spoken word meaning 'go,' etc.

Second, there are writing systems in which the written symbols refer to SOUNDS and therefore have PHONOLOGICAL REFERENCE. One would like to call such systems PHONOGRAPHIC ("sound writing"), but unfortunately this term has already been claimed for quite a different use. Systems of this type fall into two subclasses. In most of them the phonological unit symbolized is the PHONEME; such a system is called ALPHABETIC, and the set of symbols constitutes the ALPHABET. Our own writing system is essentially of this sort, though there are some unfortunate complications which we shall discuss shortly. In a second type of writing system the phonological unit symbolized is the SYLLABLE; such a system is called SYLLABIC, and the set of symbols constitutes the SYLLABARY. Japanese offers a good example; we shall describe it in a moment.

These two basic types of writing systems—logographic and "phonographic"—differ enormously in their advantages and disadvantages, as well as in the learning problems involved. A logographic system has the delightful advantage that a given written symbol can be read one way in one area and another way in another area (just as the logographic symbol 8 can be read "eight" in English, "huit" in French, "ocho" in Spanish, "vós'em' " in Russian, etc.). This includes not only such minor differences as using a given character which you pronounce "tomayto" and I pronounce "tomahto"; it can also include, with complete ease, a character which you pronounce "pail" and I pronounce "bucket." This characteristic of the logographic system is highly useful in China, where local speech varies enormously from one locality to another. (Indeed, it is only by the grossest sort of exaggeration that we can say that a single language "Chinese" is spoken throughout the whole area.) At the same time, a logographic system has one extremely serious disadvantage—so serious that Communist China is working on plans to shift over to an alphabetic system: to become fully literate one has to learn thousands of characters, and this quite literally takes many years of learning. The problem is somewhat mitigated by the fact that the system does not use, say, 20,000 totally *different* characters (which would present a truly insuperable learning problem), but a relatively small set of basic characters out of which compound characters are constructed. Nevertheless, the learning problem is a staggering one.

If you are studying a language with a logographic writing system, you should consider the language and the writing system as totally different learning problems. Learn the language itself with the aid of some sort of alphabetic notation. (Your textbook will almost certainly provide this. If it does not, throw the book away; it is of no use to you.) Once you have a fair control over the language, you can then study the writing system just as you might study the art, history, or politics of the country. But do so *only* after you have learned a considerable amount of the language itself. In giving these warnings, we do not mean to frighten you away from learning the writing system or from learning a language which uses such a writing system. Once you are properly prepared for it, you—like most people—will probably find a logographic writing system fascinating. For one thing, properly drawn characters can bring great esthetic pleasure. For another, one gets a kind of secret joy out of being able to read and write such exotic looking things.

In a logographic writing system there are two levels of symbolic structure: (1) a written symbol denotes a spoken word; and then (2) the spoken word denotes some sort of object, action, quality, etc. In a "phonographic" writing system there are three levels of symbolic structure: (1) a written symbol denotes a phoneme (or, in a syllabary, a syllable); (2) one or more phonemes (or syllables) form a spoken word; and then (3) the spoken word denotes some sort of object, action, quality, etc.

An alphabetic writing system obviously requires, at most, only as many symbols ("letters") as there are phonemes in the language, and these are always very few in number. If we count only consonants and vowels (including diphthongs), American Spanish has 22 phonemes, Italian has 23, Castilian Spanish 24, French 36, German 38, a common variety of American English 38, Russian 39, and British English 40. (These figures are only approximate, since different phonemic analyses are possible in most cases.) Learning these small numbers of symbols is a very simple matter indeed. Furthermore, the number of necessary symbols can be reduced somewhat if the writing system provides for "compound symbols."

In English, for example, instead of using special symbols for the initial consonants of /čin šin θin/ our writing system uses the compound symbols *ch, sh, th: chin, shin, thin.*

A syllabic writing system obviously requires more symbols than an alphabetic one, since every language has more syllables than it has phonemes. In English, where (letting "V" stand for vowel and "C" for consonant) our syllable types run all the way from simple "V" (*a, I*) to such complicated things as "CCCVCCC" (*sprints*) and "CCVCCCC" (*glimpsed*), a syllabic writing system would be catastrophic: there would be an intolerable number of symbols to learn. But if a language has only a few syllable types, a syllabic writing system may be very efficient and easy to learn. Japanese offers a good example. Here there are only three common syllable types, namely (1) "V," e.g. /i e a o u/; (2) "CV," e.g. /ki ke ka ko ku/, /ni ne na no nu/; and (3) "CyV," e.g. /kya kyo kyu/, /nya nyo nyu/. Examples: *Yo-ko-ha-ma, Na-ga-sa-ki, Hi-ro-hi-to, Fu-ji-ya-ma, To-o-kyo-o.* The Japanese have therefore been able to develop a very simple syllabary in which (1) there is a special symbol for every syllable of the type "V" (/i e a o u/); (2) there is a special symbol for every syllable of the type "CV" (/ki ke ka ko ku/ etc.); and (3) syllables of the type "CyV" (/kya kyo kyu/ etc.) are written as if they were "Ci + yV" (/ki + ya ki + yo ki + yu/ etc.). Hence *Yokohama, Nagasaki, Hirohito, Fujiyama* are written with four symbols each; and *Tokyo* (actually *To-o-kyo-o*) is written with five symbols (as if it were *To-o-ki-yo-o*). Because the language has so few syllable types, only a small number of syllabic symbols are required and the whole system can be learned in a few hours. (Unfortunately the Japanese complicate this very efficient system by using two different syllabaries, which are in part quite dissimilar, and by using one of them along with many thousands of Chinese characters.)

The advantages and disadvantages of an alphabet or a syllabary are precisely the opposite of those which we found in logographic writing. If you say "tomayto" and I say "tomahto," then either (1) you must write the word your way and I must write it my way, or (2) we both write it the same way but pronounce it differently—though this immediately begins to detract from the advantages of a "phonographic" type of writing system. If you say "pail" where I say "bucket," however, we have little choice: you will write your word and I must learn it, and I will write my word and you must learn it. To work efficiently, a writing system with phonological reference must be used in a language which is more or less uniform both phonologically (in the phonemic shapes of its words) and lexically (in the words it uses). A striking phenomenon of the past several centuries has been the development of large numbers of "standard languages" which meet precisely these conditions.

Compared with these few disadvantages, the advantages of a phonological writing system are enormous. Instead of thousands and thousands of characters and their referents, one must learn only (1) a tiny number of symbols (26 in our alphabet), plus (2) the rules for using these symbols to refer to phonemes or syllables. Though these rules may be quite inconsistent and complicated, so that the system begins to take on some of the characteristics of a logographic system (note how we distinguish the words *pear, pair, pare,* all $=$ /pḗr/, by symbolizing the phoneme /ē/ in three different ways), the learning problem is still insignificant when compared to that of learning thousands of characters. Furthermore, there is another enormous advantage: if you come upon a written word which you have never seen before, there is a very high percentage of probability that you will know how to pronounce it and hence be able to use it in speech. (The words *pear, pair, pare* will surely all begin with /p/ and end with /r/, and the vowel can hardly be that of *par, pore, poor,* or *purr.*)

A remark needs to be made at this point about alphabets other than our own. Though the alphabet was invented only once, it has developed in many different ways in many different parts of the world. The student who wants to learn Greek must therefore learn the Greek alphabet, the student who wants to learn Russian must learn the Cyrillic alphabet, the student who wants to learn Arabic must learn the Arabic alphabet (with its, to us, odd swirls and dots), the student who wants to learn Hindi must learn the Devanagari syllabary-alphabet (it is a bit of a cross between the two), and so on. Many students look upon the learning of such a new alphabet as a task of heroic proportions; and once they have more or less learned, say, Cyrillic, they boast that they "know" Russian. Still others are frightened away from learning one of these languages because "I would have to learn a new alphabet." Both of these attitudes are preposterous. The student who knows Cyrillic does not necessarily know any Russian at all; and the student who cannot spare an hour or two to learn the 32 symbols of the Cyrillic alphabet will surely not have the patience to spend 200 hours or more gaining an elementary knowledge of Russian. Some alphabets *do* take longer to learn than an hour or two, and all of them require many hours of practice before one can read them fluently. Compared with learning a new language, however, learning a new alphabet requires only an insignificant amount of time and effort.

The extent to which a "phonographic" writing system (alphabetic or syllabic) agrees with the phonological system of the language with which it is used is called the FIT of the writing system. If in an alphabetic system there is a one-to-one correspondence between phonemes and written letters, so that each letter always represents the same phoneme and each phoneme is always written with the same letter, the fit is 100%. The English writing system would have perfect fit if it contained only such items as *in, pin, spin, spits, hen, bend, spent, crests, at, sand, cast, straps, hot, crop, flop, spots*, etc. The introduction of compound symbols (such as *ch, sh, th*) does not in any way destroy this perfect fit as long as such symbols remain unambiguous—e.g. so long as there are no spellings such as *chaos* (where *ch* = /k/), *gashouse* (where *sh* = /s + h/), and *then* (where *th* = /ð/ rather than the usual /θ/ of *thin*). If the fit of our writing system were really perfect, a person who already knew English could easily learn both the few symbols involved and their constant phonemic reference. He could then spell any word he knew how to pronounce, and he could read and pronounce any word he saw spelled whether he had previously known it or not. Note that we say this could be done by a person *who already knew English*. A foreign learner would still have to struggle with the interference produced by the sound system and the writing system of his native language. Still, even he would have a relatively simple task in merely learning the new writing system.

Languages with writing systems that have very good fit are popularly described as "phonetic languages." This is a rather unfortunate expression, since it confuses "language" with "writing system." (A writing system *symbolizes* a language; it is not itself the language.) Furthermore, the word *phonetic* means 'pertaining to the sounds of speech,' so that all languages are by definition "phonetic." Nevertheless, the point is clear: in such a language the correspondence between sound and spelling is very good, and the writing system presents no really difficult learning problems. Excellent fit of this sort is likely to be found with languages for which new alphabetic systems have recently been devised, as is the case with Turk-ish, or with languages whose speakers have repeatedly and system-atically revised the spelling system so as to produce better fit, as is the case with Dutch. Children who grow up using such languages can learn to read and write them very easily, without having to study spelling for years and years in school as we do; and foreign learners benefit correspondingly.

If it is possible for some languages to have such good fit be-tween sound and spelling, why is it that other languages (like Eng-lish) have such notoriously bad fit? There seem to be three main reasons. First, since the alphabet was invented only once, speakers ever since then have started out trying to write their language in a borrowed alphabet which perhaps did not contain enough letters (e.g. 26 letters whereas the language had perhaps 35 phonemes), or which did not contain letters which matched some of their pho-nemes properly (e.g. English /θ/ and /š/), or which was most likely deficient in both respects. Second, even if the speakers do manage to work out a writing system of some sort, they may then in the course of time borrow large numbers of words from one or more foreign languages and insist on keeping the foreign spellings unchanged (as we have borrowed Greek words in such Latinized spellings as *psyche* and *ptomaine*). Finally, and perhaps most im-portantly, the sound systems of all languages change in the course of time, often drastically, so that what was a reasonable fit at one time is a most unreasonable fit three, four, or five hundred years later. If the speakers then insist on keeping the writing system essentially unchanged (as we have done in English since about the time of Chaucer), the result is a very poor fit indeed.

We can illustrate this last point from the history of English, and at the same time clear up a matter which puzzles many people when they first note the strikingly different ways in which vowels are written in English and in other languages using the Latin alpha-bet. In the 14th century, at the time of Chaucer, English had the following short and long vowels:

			Long		
			(1) rīde(n)	'to ride'
Short			(2) fēde(n)	'to feed'
(1) bidde(n)	'to bid'		(3) rę̄de(n)	'to read'
(2) bedde	'bed'		(4) fāde(n)	'to fade'
(3) badde	'bad'			

(4) god	'god'	(5) rǫd	'road'
(5) budde	'bud'	(6) fōde	'food'
		(7) loud	'loud'

Most of the long vowel symbols had what are often called the "continental values" of these letters, that is, pronunciations much like those given to the same letters in many languages of continental Europe. Long vowel (1) apparently sounded much like that of modern *need,* long vowel (2) much like that of modern *made,* (3) like modern *fair,* (4) like modern *father,* (5) like modern *sawed,* (6) like modern *code,* and (7) like modern *mood.* (The spelling *ou* in *loud* had been borrowed from French, where it still symbolizes a vowel sound similar to that of English *mood.*) Then, not long afterwards, in what is called the "Great English Vowel Shift," the pronunciations of the long vowels began to change gradually to the sounds which we now use in these words. The spellings, however, were in general *not* changed. As a result, of the languages which use the Latin alphabet, English now stands alone in the general phonetic values which it gives to the vowel letters of such words as *ride, feed, fade, food, loud.*

The short vowels also changed in pronunciation, though less spectacularly. Short vowels (1) and (2) apparently sounded, even in Chaucer's time, much like the vowels of modern *bid* and *bed.* But short vowel (3), then sounding much like that of modern *nod,* changed to its present sound in *bad;* short vowel (4), then much like that of modern *sawed* (though shorter), changed to its present sound in *god;* and short vowel (5), then much like that of modern *good,* changed in some surroundings to its present sound in *bud.* (In other surroundings it seems to have remained more or less unchanged, cf. modern *put, push, bush,* etc.). As a result, English again stands alone in the general "short values" which it gives to the letters *a, o, u* in *bad, god, bud,* etc.

The examples in the above table also explain another peculiarity of English spelling: the fact that we have so many words in which a final *-e* does not represent a corresponding phoneme in the modern pronunciation. The final *-n*'s of the above words were already being lost in Middle English times; that is why we have here placed them in parentheses. The final *-e*'s were being dropped in pronunciation in some positions, and they were dropped altogether (in pronunciation!) during the following centuries. In spelling, however, the final *-e*'s were either kept or dropped according to a rather devious but nevertheless effective scheme which we can call the "principle of indirect symbolization." In modern *bid*, for example, we have dropped the letter *-e* which was written (and pronounced) in Middle English; here the modern *absence* of a final letter *-e* indicates that the preceding *i* represents the phoneme /i/. In modern *ride*, on the other hand, we have kept the letter *-e* which was written (and pronounced) in Middle English; here the modern *presence* of a final letter *-e* symbolizes, indirectly, the fact that the preceding letter *i* represents not /i/ but the modern phoneme /ai/. Compare also such pairs of words as *met* vs. *mete, fad* vs. *fade, rod* vs. *rode, tub* vs. *tube.* This "principle of indirect symbolization" is roundabout and devious; but it is also highly effective, since it allows us to use the five letters *i, e, a, o, u* to symbolize not just *five* vowel phonemes (those of *rid, met, fad, rod, tub*), but no less than *ten* vowel phonemes (the preceding five plus those of *ride, mete, fade, rode, tube*). In accordance with this principle, the letter *-e* has been added in modern spelling to many words which never had a final phoneme /-e/ in either Middle or Old English, cf. modern *tide, rode* from Old English *tīd, rād.* Unfortunately, the usefulness of this ingenious device is greatly impaired by the fact that our spelling system uses it so inconsistently. The phoneme /ai/, for example, is not only symbolized by the spelling *i—e (ride, side, hide, wide*, etc.) but also by such spellings as *night, height, aisle,* etc. In addition, we have many examples of final written *-e* where it does *not* signal a special value of the preceding vowel: *to live, to give, to love, the dove, to move,* etc.

The "principle of indirect symbolization" is important because the learner is likely to encounter it in any language which is written alphabetically. Here is a Dutch example:

Short vowel:

| redden | 'to save' | tallen | 'numbers' | potten | 'pots' |

Long vowel:

| reden | 'reason' | talen | 'languages' | poten | 'paws' |

Dutch has no phonemically double consonant phonemes such as /dd/, /ll/, /tt/. This being the case, it is free to use double consonant *letters* for some other purpose. It uses them as an indirect method of indicating that a preceding vowel is short, as in the first row above. Correspondingly, it uses a *single* consonant letter in such positions to serve as an indirect indication of the fact that the preceding vowel is long. In one-syllable words Dutch uses a direct method of symbolization: short vowels are symbolized by a single vowel letter, as in *tal* 'number,' *pot* 'pot'; long vowels are symbolized (among other ways) by a doubled vowel letter: *taal* 'language,' *poot* 'paw.' Though this combination of direct and indirect symbolizations at first strikes one as needlessly complicated, it is actually a very economical and unambiguous way of symbolizing the fact that one has short vowels in such singular and plural forms as *tal, tallen,* and *pot, potten,* but long vowels in such singular and plural forms as *taal, talen,* and *poot, poten.*

Russian offers a particularly striking example of "indirect symbolization." The language has 5 vowel phonemes and 34 consonant phonemes. A writing system with perfect fit would therefore need to have 39 different symbols. However, of the 34 consonant phonemes there are 24 which fall into two matchings sets: 12 plain (traditionally called "hard") and 12 palatalized (traditionally called "soft"). Instead of using 24 different letters to represent these 24 different consonant phonemes, the Russian writing system uses only 12 different letters and symbolizes the difference between plain and palatalized indirectly by using two sets of vowel letters: 5 to indicate that a preceding consonant is plain, and 5 to indicate that a preceding consonant is palatalized. There are complications: among other things, a special "soft sign" is needed for cases where a "soft consonant" is not followed by a vowel. Nevertheless, it is essentially true to say that this ingenious system of indirect symbolization permits Russian to use an alphabet of only 32 symbols for a language which has 39 phonemes.

Because in alphabetic writing systems the letters of the alphabet symbolize the phonemes of the language, it might at first glance seem that a writing system with perfect fit should always show a one-to-one correspondence between letters on the one hand and phonemes on the other. This is not necessarily the case, however. Under certain conditions it may be more desirable to allow a given letter to symbolize two phonemes, just as long as the symbolization is in each case unambiguous. Consider the following examples from German:

Meaning	Phonemics		Spelling	
	'wheel'	'advice'	'wheel'	'advice'
Nominative-accusative	/rā́t/	/rā́t/	Rad	Rat
Dative (long form)	/rā́də/	/rā́tə/	Rade	Rate
Dative (short form)	/rā́t/	/rā́t/	Rad	Rat
Genitive (long form)	/rā́dəs/	/rā́təs/	Rades	Rates
Genitive (short form)	/rā́ts/	/rā́ts/	Rads	Rats

Here the morpheme meaning 'advice' shows a constant phonemic shape, namely /rā́t/. But the morpheme meaning 'wheel' shows what is called MORPHOPHONEMIC ALTERNATION, namely an alternation in phonemic shape between /rā́t/ with /t/ and /rā́d/ with /d/. This particular alternation is automatic in German: any stem-final /d/ before vowel (/rā́d-ə/, /rā́d-əs/) alternates automatically with /t/ word-finally (/rā́t/) and before /s/ (/rā́t-s/). Accordingly, if we take the shape /rā́d/ as basic, we can predict the occurrence of the shape /rā́t/ with complete certainty. The regular German orthography takes advantage of this fact and uses a spelling with the letter *d* in all forms: *Rad, Rade, Rades, Rads*. Such a morphophonemic type of spelling has two advantages. First, it makes it possible to spell the morpheme meaning 'wheel' the same way in all forms, and thus to distinguish it in all forms from *Rat* 'advice.' Second, it shows that the word *Rat* will keep its /t/ in the longer dative and genitive forms, but that the word *Rad* will change its /t/ to /d/. For the reader, there is still a perfect fit between writing and language: word-finally and before *s* the letter *d* can stand only for the phoneme /t/, never for /d/, since the rules of the German phonological code do not allow /d/ to occur in these two positions. For the writer the fit is no longer perfect: he must know that the /t/ of /rā́t/ 'wheel' changes to /d/ before vowels, and is therefore to be written *d;* whereas the /t/ of /rā́t/ 'advice' remains unchanged in all forms and is therefore to be written *t.* That is to say, the writer must know the language; but he must of course know the language in any case, since otherwise he could not even attempt to write it.

These same two words have the following plural forms and spellings: /rḗdər/ *Räder* and /rḗtə/ *Räte*. These spellings illustrate a feature that is relatively rare in alphabetical writing systems: the use of a special morphophonemic symbol, namely *ä*. As far as phonemic reference is concerned, this letter *ä* is (for most speakers) in every way identical with the letter *e:* before a single consonant letter it denotes long /ē/, before a double consonant letter short /e/. It has the special advantage, however, of reminding the reader that the morphemes in question have other forms containing either long /ā/ or short /a/.

Russian shows even more striking examples of morphophonemic spelling:

	Phonetics	Spelling	Meaning
Singular	[górət]	górod	'city'
Plural	[gərădá]	gorodá	'cities'
Phrase	[zá gərət]	zá gorod	'beyond the city'

Here again, as in German, there is an automatic alternation between /d/ before vowel vs. /t/ in word-final position. Russian spelling therefore uses the letter *d* quite unambiguously throughout. In addition, there is automatic alternation among the vowels [o], [ă], and [ə]: [o] occurs only in a stressed syllable, [ă] occurs only immediately preceding a stressed syllable, and [ə] occurs only in other positions. Accordingly, Russian spelling quite unambiguously uses the spelling *gorod* throughout, even though the phone [o] can never occur simultaneously in both syllables of the word, and even though it sometimes occurs in neither. The only flaw in this ingenious system is the fact that Russian spelling does not normally show which syllable is stressed; but a fluent speaker of course knows this anyhow.

As an illustration of morphophonemic spelling combined with indirect symbolization, we may cite the example of French adjectives already mentioned in Chapter 6:

Masculine		Feminine		Meaning
/grã/	grand	/grãd/	grande	'big'
/lɔ̃/	long	/lɔ̃g/	longue	'long'
/ba/	bas	/bas/	basse	'low'
/pəti/	petit	/pətit/	petite	'little'
/kur/	court	/kurt/	courte	'short'

In the first two words the letter *n* is used to symbolize indirectly the fact that the preceding vowel is nasalized; *n* always functions this way when it is followed by another consonant or stands at the end of a word. This means that French does not need to have special letters for its four nasalized vowels /ɛ̃ œ̃ ɔ̃ ã/ but can write them as *in, un, on,* and *en/an,* respectively—a saving of four letters of the alphabet. In the masculine column the spellings are morphophonemic. They show the longer forms which each morpheme will have in the feminine, and at the same time they indicate quite unambiguously the phonemic shape of the masculine through a rule which we might phrase as: "Word-final consonant letter symbolizes phonemic zero." The feminine column shows another example of indirect symbolization. Though the final letter *-e* does not represent any phoneme in ordinary pronunciation, it serves graphically to keep the preceding consonant letter out of word-final position, so that it now *does* symbolize a phoneme. A few minor adjustments have to be made when this *-e* is added: a *u* (which does not represent any phoneme in this position) must be added in *longue,* since *longe* would represent phonemic /lɔ̃ž/; and the *s* of *basse* has to be doubled, since *base* would represent phonemic /baz/. Though this ingenious combination of morphophonemic spelling and indirect symbolization is far from perfect (there are a number of unfortunate irregularities which we have not mentioned), as a practical spelling system it is probably a good deal better than a straight phonemic transcription would be. This is true, of course, only if one already knows French. We must emphasize again the fact that all normal writing systems are intended only for those who already know the language in question; they were not designed to meet the needs of those who are *learning* the language.

Before we leave the topic of writing, we need to mention one final matter. Every decade or so some enthusiast comes forth with a new "phonetic alphabet" which, he claims, will allow us to solve all the world's language problems in one fell swoop. No longer will we need to labor for countless days at the writing system of, say, Russian; the new alphabet will tell us at a glance how everything is to be pronounced, and we shall be able to learn the language in a matter of hours. Not only that: once we have mastered this new alphabet, we shall be able to learn any other language with almost no effort at all. All the present barriers to international communication and understanding will be overcome with ease, and the world will be able to live in peace and harmony forever after.

Though one hates to disillusion such earnest and honest enthusiasts, they suffer from hopeless misunderstandings. They confuse writing with language, and assume that a knowledge of the former automatically gives us a knowledge of the latter. And they assume that language consists only of sound, which their new alphabet will now immediately reveal to us. But this is clearly quite wrong. All of us are able to hear all the sound there is in any spoken message in a foreign language. Merely hearing this sound—whether directly or, through a "phonetic alphabet," indirectly—is not even the beginning of foreign-language learning. To learn the language, we must learn how to *decode* this sound phonologically, grammatically, and semantically; and this is best done by also learning how to *encode* it semantically, grammatically, and phonologically. It is indeed a shame that the "fit" between many writing systems and the languages they symbolize is so poor. Except in the case of logographic systems, however, the task of learning a writing system is relatively insignificant compared with the task of learning the language itself.

Appendix

A Bibliography of Useful Books

A. Books on linguistics. During recent years a number of useful introductions to linguistics have been written. Of the following seven, the first six are all of approximately the same level of difficulty. The seventh, though by no means difficult, is somewhat more advanced and covers a wider range of topics.

Bolinger, Dwight. *Aspects of Language*. New York: Harcourt, Brace & World, 1968. Pp. viii, 326.

Fromkin, Victoria, and Robert Rodman. *An Introduction to Language*. New York: Holt, Rinehart & Winston, 1974. Pp. vi, 357.

Langacker, Ronald W. *Language and its Structure: Some Fundamental Linguistic Concepts*. 2nd ed. New York: Harcourt Brace Jovanovich, 1973. Pp. ix, 275.

Lehmann, Winfred P. *Descriptive Linguistics: An Introduction*. New York: Random House, 1972. Pp. x, 291.

Southworth, Franklin C., and Chander J. Daswani. *Founda-*

tions of Linguistics. New York: The Free Press; London: Collier Macmillan, 1974. Pp. vi, 362.

Wardhaugh, Ronald. *Introduction to Linguistics.* New York: McGraw-Hill, 1972. Pp. viii, 239.

Lyons, John. *Introduction to Theoretical Linguistics.* Cambridge: University Press, 1968. Pp. x, 519.

The above seven books all give a "modern" view of linguistics. They include the exciting advances (or so most linguists believe) that were made during the late 1950's and the 1960's—advances begun by Noam Chomsky and his "transformational-generative grammar" and continued by many other scholars. At the same time, there are a few older works that are timeless classics and that are still worth reading today. Outstanding among these is the following book. This may well be the most readable and stimulating introduction to linguistics that has ever been written:

Sapir, Edward. *Language.* New York: Harcourt, Brace, 1921. Pp. vii, 258. Reprinted as a paperback: Harvest Books No. HB7, 1955.

B. Books on phonetics. (For the phonetics of German, Italian, and Spanish, see Section C.)

Malmberg, Bertil. *Phonetics.* New York: Dover Publications, 1963. Pp. iv, 123.—Written by an internationally known Swedish phonetician and adapted from the original French version of 1954. Simply written, easy to read, and—as far as it goes—an excellent introduction to all aspects of phonetics. But the presentation is often all too brief, and it is largely limited to the sounds of a few familiar European languages.

Pike, Kenneth L. *Phonetics.* Ann Arbor: University of Michigan Press, 1943. Pp. ix, 182.—Part II (pp. 83 ff.) gives an excellent presentation of the basic principles of articulatory phonetics. It provides a framework for describing and understanding all the types of sounds that the human vocal apparatus can produce.

Heffner, R-M. S. *General Phonetics.* Madison: University of Wisconsin Press, 1950. Pp. xvii, 253.—Though this book contains far more technical details than the average language learner will want or need, it also presents a wealth of useful information for any language learner, especially in Part Two, "The Sounds of Speech."

C. Contrastive Structure Series. The volumes in this series have been sponsored by the Center for Applied Linguistics, Arlington, Virginia. Their purpose has been to highlight the contrasts between the linguistic structures of English and of the five foreign languages most commonly taught in the United States: French, German, Italian, Russian, and Spanish. Though these studies have been written primarily for use by foreign language teachers, they contain a great deal of information that will be of help to the adult language learner who has the time and courage to tackle them. The following volumes in this series have been published by the University of Chicago Press:

German: William G. Moulton, *The Sounds of English and German,* 1962, pp. xiii, 145. Herbert L. Kufner, *The Grammatical Structures of English and German,* 1962, pp. xi, 95.

Italian: Frederick B. Agard and Robert J. Di Pietro, *The Sounds of English and Italian,* 1965, pp. vii, 76. The same, *The Grammatical Structures of English and Italian,* 1965, pp. vii, 91.

Spanish: Robert P. Stockwell and J. Donald Bowen, *The Sounds of English and Spanish,* 1965, pp. xi, 168. Robert P. Stockwell, J. Donald Bowen, and John W. Martin, *The Grammatical Structures of English and Spanish,* 1965, pp. xi, 328.

D. Books on language learning.

Nida, Eugene A. *Learning a Foreign Language: A Handbook for Missionaries.* New York: Committee on Missionary Personnel, Foreign Missions Conference of North America, 1950. Pp. ix, 237. —Though intended for missionaries in the field, this book can be read with great profit by any adult language learner. It presents the principles of linguistic analysis in clear and readable fashion; it is particularly helpful for someone learning a language for which there are available none of the customary learning aids such as textbooks, grammars, dictionaries, etc.

Politzer, Robert L. *Foreign Language Learning: A Linguistic Introduction.* Preliminary edition. Englewood Cliffs, N.J.: Prentice-Hall, 1965. Pp. ix, 155.—Addressed primarily to school and college students of foreign languages. The book discusses the basic problems of language learning and includes many exercises.

The following two books were the great classics on language learning and language teaching two and three generations ago.

Both of them still make valuable reading for the language learner. Palmer's book, in particular, is strikingly "modern." Indeed, much of the recent "revolution" in language teaching in the United States could be described as a return to the principles which Palmer laid down half a century ago.

Sweet, Henry. *The Practical Study of Languages: A Guide for Teachers and Learners.* London: Oxford University Press, 1964 (original edition 1899). Pp. xv, 176.

Palmer, Harold E. *The Principles of Language-Study.* London: Oxford University Press, 1964 (original edition 1917). Pp. ix, 142.

Index

direct object 73
distributional problems 59-60
duality principle 30-31
Dutch 21, 51, 55, 98-99, 106, 110, 125, 127-128

ear 34, 39
elliptical sentence 67
embedding 28, 67-68, 74, 85-86
enclitic 97, 105
encoding, *see* grammatical encoding, phonological encoding, semantic encoding
ending = inflectional suffix 93-94
equational sentence 74
Eskimo 104

feedback 34
filler (of a grammatical slot) 73
fit (of a phonographic writing system) 124-125, 128, 132
flapped *r* 54, 56
flapped *t* 54, 56
form 27; *see also* bound form, free form, full form, plain form, polite form
free form 87
French 4, 7, 16, 17, 25, 51, 52, 54, 55, 60, 82, 83, 96, 98, 103, 105, 109, 110, 120, 121, 126, 130-131
full form 81
function word 43, 73, 74, 89, 91, 102

gender 13, 16, 17, 71, 75, 109-110
general question 78-79
genitive case 11, 72, 74
German 24, 25, 51, 54, 55, 60, 83, 103, 109, 110, 115-116, 121, 128-130, 135
glide (of a vowel) 56
glottal stop 58
government 72, 75
grammar 16-17, 26-28, 65-86, *passim*
grammatical decoding 23, 42-44, 45-47
grammatical encoding 23, 26-28, 33-34
grammatical function 72
grammatical meaning 88, 92, 101, 102, 107-113, 115, 116
Great English Vowel Shift 126
Greek 26, 29, 93, 95, 97, 123, 125
guessing 18, 20, 115
gum ridge 51, 54, 55-56, 57

head (of a construction) 71, 74, 88
hierarchical order 74, 77
Hindi 75, 123

IC, *see* immediate constituent

Ilocano 94, 95, 103, 105-106
imitation 49-50, 53, 54, 55, 58
immediate constituent 69, 70, 71, 74, 76, 87
imperative 81
inanimate gender 71, 109, 110
independent clause, *see* main clause
Indian (American) languages 62, 110
indirect object 73
indirect symbolization 127-128, 130-131
Indonesian 51
infix 94, 95
inflection 26, 88, 93, 94, 95, 96
interjection 90
intonation 53, 66, 107
Italian 55, 56, 103, 121, 135

Jabberwocky 42-43, 44, 88-89, 91, 102
Japanese 7, 10-11, 58, 74, 82, 83, 104, 111, 120, 122

kinship terms 106-107

l sounds 7, 55
Latin 9-13, 26, 72, 83, 94, 103, 109 110, 125
letter 121, 124, 126-129, 131
linguistic geography 41
linguistic reference 118
linking *r* 98
liquid 58
logic, language and 2, 8-9, 104
logographic writing system 119-123, 132

main clause 67, 68
matrix sentence 85
meaning 24-26, 42, 88, 101-116, *passim; see also* denotative meaning, connotative meaning, constructional meaning, grammatical meaning
mimicry 2, 49, 52
modification 71, 90, 107, 108, 110
monitoring 34
mood 71, 112-113
morpheme 26-27, 29-33, *passim*
morphological reference 120
morphologically determined morpheme shape 33
morphology 27
morphophonemic 129-131
motor memory 15
music, language and 22

nasalized vowel 51, 130-131

105, 120, 121, **135**
specific question 79
speech 29, *passim*
speech organs 29, 35-38, 50, 56
spelling 125, 126, 129, 130; *see also*
 writing
square brackets [ ] 36
standard language 123
statement 61, 78-79
stem 92-95
storage device 34, 45
stress 60-61, 63, 92, 95, 130
stress-timed rhythm 63
structural description 70
structural diagram 70, 71, 73, 77
subject 70, 88, 107-108, *passim*
subordinate clause 67, 68, 84-86
subordination 84-86
subordinating conjunction 68, 90
substitute word 81, 90-91, 109, 110
subtraction 96
suffix 43, 93-94, 95, 110, 111
suprafix 94-95
surface structure 77-86, 107-108
syllabary 120-122
syllabic writing system, 120, 122, 124
syllable 120, 122, *passim*
syllable-timed rhythm 63-64
symbol 117-122, 124
synonym 114, 115
syntax 27

tense 12, 71, 80, 112
third person singular present morpheme
 32
timing 53, 62-64
tone 62, 94-95

tone language 62
tongue-tip *r* 51, 54
transformation 28, 44, 68, 77-86, 90,
 107-108
transformational grammar 107-108
transitive 46
translation 18-20, 115-116
trilled *r* 54
Turkish 125

ultimate constituent 69
unstressed vowel 58-59, 59-60
uvular *r* 4, 51, 54

verb 74-75, 88, 91, 93, *passim; see also*
 auxiliary verb
vocabulary 18
vocal cords 55
vocative case 11
voice (active, passive) 113
voiced 32, 55, 97, 98-99
voiceless 32, 55, 97, 98-99
vowel 56, 121, 122, 125-128, *passim;*
 see also unstressed vowel, nasalized
 vowel
VP = verb phrase 69-74

word 26-27, 69, 87, 119-120, *passim;*
 see also content word, function
 word, nuisance word, substitute
 word
word field 114
word order 26, 43, 72, 74-75, 78, 82,
 107
word stress 60, 61
writing 13-16, 117-132

X-ray moving pictures 35